Out of the Ordinary

OTHER BOOKS BY DAVID ROPER

A Burden Shared

Elijah: A Man Like Us

Growing Slowly Wise

In Quietness and Confidence

Jacob: The Fools God Chooses

A Man to Match the Mountain

Psalm 23: The Song of a Passionate Heart

The Strength of a Man

Discovery House Publishers

Books, music, and videos that feed the soul with the Word of God

Box 3566 Grand Rapids, MI 49501

God's Hand at Work in Everyday Lives

Out of the Ordinary

David Roper

Discovery House Publishers is affiliated with RBC Ministries,
Grand Rapids, Michigan 49512

Discovery House books are distributed to the trade exclusively by
Barbour Publishing, Inc., Uhrichsville, Ohio 44683

Book Design: Sherri L. Hoffman

Library of Congress Cataloging-in-Publication Data

Roper, David, 1933—
    Out of the ordinary : God's hand at work in everyday lives / by David
Roper.
        p.   cm.
    ISBN 1-57293-107-8
    1. Meditations. 2. Bible—Meditations. I. Title.
    BV4832.3.R66 2003
    242—dc21

                                                    2003000262

Printed in the United States of America

03 04 05 06 07 08 09 /DP/ 10 9 8 7 6 5 4 3 2 1

Contents

Introduction

Read, sweet, how others strove,
    till we are stouter . . .
Brave names of men
    and celestial women,
Passed out of record
    into renown!
        —EMILY DICKINSON

Saint Ambrose, Augustine's mentor, said we should "have a good reason for beginning, and our end should be within due limits." Good advice for preachers and writers, I say.

My "reason for beginning" is to impart a few thoughts that have come my way as a result of my own spiritual reading. I initially put them on paper for a group of men with whom I've gathered on Wednesday mornings for mutual encouragement and spiritual enrichment for twenty-five years. Now I offer them to you for your consideration.

The essays that follow come in all sizes, but I trust that with each the end is within "due limits," and that I stopped writing before I ran out of anything worthwhile to say. I leave that to your judgment.

Each study is based on a biblical character, some of whom are well-known, while others are "well-known for being unknown," as a friend of mine once said. But known or unknown, the men and women who fill my thoughts and these pages were ordinary people, so ordinary that were it not for the fact that God worked in their circumstances for His purposes, their stories would be forgotten, without record, lost to history.

Yet their stories endure, and in them we catch a glimpse of the holy work God is doing in and around commonplace men and women. For it is "out of the ordinary" that God's extraordinary work is done.

David Roper
Boise, Idaho

A Friend of Souls

There are hermit souls that live withdrawn
In the peace of their self-content;
There are souls, like stars, that dwell apart
In a fellowless firmament;
There are pioneer souls that blaze their paths
Where highways never ran;
But let me live by the side of the road,
And be a friend to man.
—SAMUEL WALTER FOSS[1]

WARM-UP: *Genesis 14:18–20*

*C*onsider Abraham, returning from a raid on King Kedorlaomer and a coalition of Mesopotamian armies—battle-scarred, exhausted, and fearful, well aware that he has angered four of the most powerful kings of his day.[2] As he trudges through the Valley of Shaveh, Melchizedek, King of Salem, brings out bread and wine and *blesses* him.

"Without doubt the lesser person is blessed by the greater," said the writer of Hebrews (7:7), referring to this event. So who was this great high priest who blessed our great father Abraham?

Very little is known about Melchizedek—only that he was the king of Salem (ancient Jerusalem[3]), that he was a "priest of God Most High," and that he fed and blessed the famished Abraham. Yet this king-priest has been lionized in the history of Israel and the church.

Commentators make much of Melchizedek's name, which means "King of Righteousness," but it was a common throne name in those days; and the name is actually written in two parts, as though it were a title rather than a personal name.

The Essenes of Qumran thought Melchizedek was an angel. The philosopher Philo believed he was the divine *Logos*. The Jewish historian Josephus said he was only a man, but so righteous that he was "by common consent . . . made a priest of God."

David saw Melchizedek as a prototype of the promised Messiah who would establish a new order of king-priests (Psalm 110:1–4). The author of Hebrews, taking the argument further, said that Melchizedek was like Jesus, who is a priest despite His non-Levitical ancestry, whose title is "king of righteousness" and "king of peace," and who, because He appears in the account without beginning or end of life, "remains a priest *forever*" (Hebrews 7:2–3, emphasis added).

David and the writer of Hebrews have the last word, of course—Melchizedek is an Old Testament "type," or picture of Jesus. But, as Josephus correctly noted, Melchizedek was also just a man, and as such is an example of the kind of man I want to be.

I want to be a friend of souls. I want to stand by the side of the road, as Melchizedek did, waiting for weary travelers, in the places "where the ragged people go."[4] I want to look for those who have been battered and wronged by others, who carry the dreary burden of a wounded and disillusioned heart. I want to nourish and refresh them with bread and wine and send them on their way with a benediction.

I cannot "fix" those who pass my way, though I may want to; but I can love them and listen to their hearts. I can pray with them. I can share a word of Scripture with them when it's appropriate. I can sing "sustaining songs," as lovers of Winnie the Pooh do. And I can leave them with a blessing.

A "blessing" is more than a parting shibboleth or a polite response to a sneeze. We bless others when we bring them to the One who is the source of all blessing. Melchizedek blessed Abram, saying, "Blessed be Abram *by God Most High."* As Billy Graham would say, he blessed him *real good.*

To "bless" is to "bestow something that promotes or contributes to another's happiness, well-being, or prosperity." The Hebrew word comes from a root that means "to kneel," perhaps because of an ancient association between kneeling and receiving good from a benefactor.

In the Old Testament, God is the benefactor, the One who gives aid. He bestows the blessing. "This is how you are to bless the Israelites," God commanded Moses. "Say to them: 'The LORD bless you and keep you; the LORD make his face shine upon you and be gracious to you; the LORD turn his face toward you and give you peace'" (Numbers 6:24–26).

I cannot strengthen feeble hands, nor can I straighten knees that have given way, but I can bring weary travelers to the One who can. His bread offers endurance, strength, and eternal consolation. His wine gladdens and sustains the heart.

I cannot undo the cruel or dreary circumstances of anyone's journey, nor can I take away their travail, but I can remind those who trudge by that there is One who walks with them—who holds them with His right hand, who guides them with His counsel, and afterward will take them into glory.

I cannot help the helpless, but I can love them, pray with them, and bring them to the throne of grace to find help in time of need. I cannot show them the way, but I can "show them God," as theologian John Piper says.

This is my blessing. ❦

Holy Laughter

Fairy tales do not deny the existence of. . . sorrow and failure: the possibility of these is necessary to the joy of deliverance; it denies (in the face of much evidence if you will)
universal final defeat . . . giving a glimpse of Joy, Joy beyond
the walls of the world, poignant as grief.

—J. R. R. TOLKIEN

WARM-UP: *Genesis 21:1-8*

*I*t is a commonplace of Christian thought that joy is deep
tranquility. Yet it seems to me that biblical joy is something
more: it is "holy laughter"—the laughter of Sarah, for example:
"God has brought me laughter, and everyone who hears about this
will laugh with me" (Genesis 21:6).

Behind Sarah's laugh lay a promise. Twenty-five years before,
a mysterious visitor, actually God in disguise, promised Abraham
that he would have a son (Genesis 18:9–15). Sarah, eavesdropping
on the other side of the tent flap, chuckled to herself in disbelief.

Why did Sarah laugh? Was it a belly laugh over the naiveté of
men? Was it the self-deprecating laugh of one who considered
herself unworthy of God's grace? Was it a bitter laugh over the disappointment of past hopes? We are not told. What we *are* told is
that Abraham's body was dead, and, as the KJV text so quaintly puts
it, "it ceased to be with Sarah after the manner of women" (Genesis 18:11; Hebrews 11:12).

But, though it seemed impossible, the Lord did for Sarah
what He had promised: Sarah "bore a son to Abraham in his old
age, at the very time God had promised him" (Genesis 21:2). God
created new life in Sarah's dead womb—the promised seed, the

link to the One who would bring salvation to the world. And Sarah laughed again, this time the laughter of joyous surprise.

Joy is akin to humor, which, they tell me, is the sudden perception of an incongruity. A story takes an unexpected twist, jerks our minds around, and we laugh. A joke, in other words, is a "surprise."

The etymology of the word "joy" suggests a similar idea—surprise. (That's the basis of the pun in C. S. Lewis's autobiography, *Surprised by Joy.*) God sends a happy surprise and the emotion we feel is joy.

G. K. Chesterton claimed that joy, "which is the small publicity of the pagan, is the gigantic secret of the Christian ... and the dominant theme of Christian faith. By its creed (i.e., what we believe) joy becomes something gigantic and sadness something special (occasional) and small." In other words, certain things we *believe* lead us to laugh. We "get the joke."

Joy comes with a sudden perception of truth, when some word of God breaks into our minds. George MacDonald says, "[The Christian] does not take his joy from himself. He feels joy in himself, but it comes to him from God."

Joy is an "Aha!" moment, a startling revelation, a sudden awareness, an abrupt remembrance of God's goodness and grace—and we rejoice![5]

I think of a friend who spent four years and thousands of dollars pursuing a Ph.D. at a West Coast university only to be told shortly before graduation that his Christian presuppositions precluded the degree. For a moment Bob envisioned dollars and days sprouting wings and flying away. Then a truth came to mind, accompanied by the words of an old hymn:

> I'd rather have Jesus than silver or gold,
> I'd rather be His than have riches untold ...
> I'd rather have Jesus than *anything* this world affords today.

And Bob *laughed,* a clear, ringing laugh—at which point his advisor thought he'd lost his mind. But this was not insanity. Bob just "got the joke."

I think of another example, this time from C. S. Lewis's *The Lion, the Witch, and the Wardrobe.* The White Witch, with deep magic, had put Aslan to death on the Stone Table. The children, distraught at his death, wandered back to the table to mourn him, only to find that he had risen from the dead! (A *deeper* magic had brought Aslan back to life.)

> [Aslan] stood for a second, his eyes very bright, his limbs quivering, lashing himself with his tail. Then he made a leap high over their heads and landed on the other side of the Table. Laughing, though she didn't know why, Lucy scrambled over it to reach him. Aslan leaped again. A mad chase began. Round and round the hilltop he led them, now hopelessly out of their reach, now letting them almost catch his tail, now diving between them, now tossing them in the air with his huge and beautifully velveted paws and catching them again, and now stopping unexpectedly so that all three of them rolled over together in a happy laughing heap of fur and arms and legs. It was such a romp as no one has ever had, except in Narnia!

"The joy of the LORD is your strength!" Nehemiah chortles (Nehemiah 8:10). This is gigantic joy, a joy that only God and His people can know!

May our sides split with holy laughter! ❧

The Right Thing

Once you give up your integrity,
everything else is a piece of cake.
—J. R. EWING

WARM-UP: *Genesis 20*

*A*braham's lie—"She is my sister"—was his ace in the hole. Years before, the patriarch had made a deal with his wife, Sarah: if his life was ever on the line, they would lie.

Sarah was a beautiful woman, and Abraham believed that other men would covet her and kill him, which was the way things were done in those days. So he said to Sarah: "This is how you can show your love to me: Everywhere we go, say of me, 'He is my brother'" (20:13).

This was a half-truth: Sarah was Abraham's half-sister, the daughter of his father though not the daughter of his mother, as he lamely explained to King Abimelech. But it was still a lie. Sarah was his wife.

Abraham liked the lie, and he used it more than once. It was the sort of thing he could rely on when it didn't look like God was going to come through. In dire circumstances, it was Abraham's alternative to faith.

Twenty-five years before, God had promised Abraham that his "seed" would save the world. Later the promise was given to Sarah as well, though she was then barren. Now her womb had been quickened and the miracle was about to begin. (Isaac was born less than a year after this event recorded in Genesis 20.) Yet on the very brink of Isaac's conception, Abraham was about to give the would-be mother away; all of which demonstrates, I suppose, that when God's salvation finally came to earth it owed nothing to Abraham's integrity, or lack thereof, but that's another story. My interest on this occasion is King Abimelech and the integrity of *his* heart.

Abraham had pitched his tents in Philistia. Abimelech, the king of Gerar, thinking that Sarah was unmarried, took her into his harem. But before he could lay a hand on her, God appeared to him in a dream. "You're a dead man, Abimelech," He said, "for you've taken another man's wife." The king protested mightily, pleading ignorance: "I've done nothing wrong. My conscience is clear and my hands are clean. In the integrity of my heart and the innocence of my hands I have done this."

God agreed with the king and ordered him to return Sarah to her husband posthaste, which Abimelech did. But then he went one step further: he not only restored Sarah to Abraham, he also gave him sheep, oxen, servants, a thousand pieces of silver, and an offer to live in Gerar rent-free—a class act by a man who'd been lied to and dishonored.

Abimelech acted with integrity. In his heart he knew it was wrong to take another man's wife, and had he known Sarah was married, he would never have claimed her. Here was a man of the world acting in this instance with greater honor and honesty than Abraham, the man of God.

The Hebrew word translated *integrity* in our text means "wholeness," as does our English word, which comes from the same Latin root as *integer*. A person of integrity, like a whole number, is undivided, "of one piece."

Integrity means that the same ideals and absolutes govern all parts of our lives so that no part of our behavior is a lie. We do not behave one way in one setting and a different way in another. We are the same at home or away; on the job or on the road; in public or in private where no one can see what we do. Integrity is "what we are when no one is looking" (Howard Hendricks).

This means that our behavior is not governed by circumstances, conditions, or consequences, but by our decision to be true to God's Word, though that choice may cost us dearly.

Nowhere is integrity more necessary than in our marriages, for there we must be true to the truth, though the decision to do so may entail great cost. The marriage vow is not a contract that can be readily canceled by paying a penalty; it is a promise before God to love, honor, and cherish "till death do us part." Integrity means that we keep our word no matter what it costs us: we keep our oath even "when it hurts" (Psalm 15:4).

The words "for better, for worse; for richer, for poorer; in sickness and in health," take into account the possibility that keeping that promise will be difficult and that circumstances and our spouse's needs will change over time. Nevertheless, "while a normal promise indicates a determination to try, acknowledging the possibility of failure, a marriage commitment before God is a liberation from the possibility of other futures, a choice about how to spend a life that admits no second thoughts."[6]

Integrity touches marriage and *all* the bases. We must be true all the way through. That's what it means to be "whole." ❧

A Defective Leader

He has not a single redeeming defect.

—BENJAMIN DISRAELI, OF ANOTHER
BRITISH PARLIAMENTARIAN

WARM-UP: *Exodus 5:21–23*

I read somewhere that a Huey Cobra helicopter, practicing auto rotations during a military night-training exercise, landed on its tail rotor, separating the tail boom from the rest of the aircraft. Fortunately, the aircraft wound up on its skids, sliding down the runway doing 360s in a shower of sparks. As the Cobra passed the tower, the following exchange occurred:

> Tower: "Sir, do you need assistance?"
> Cobra: "I don't know, tower. We ain't done crashin' yet!"

As I look at my life and leadership over the years, I have to admit that much of it has been one resounding crack-up after another. My best-laid schemes have crashed and burned, my brilliant strategies have augured in, and I "ain't done crashin' yet."

Yet God wastes nothing—not even failure. He discerns the possibilities in every humiliating debacle and uses them to make us better leaders than we ever thought possible.

God's ways are not our ways: We equate leadership with lordship; He equates it with servanthood. We seek power so we can set things right; He strips us of importance so He can do a better job. We want strength so we can help God get on with His work; He weakens us and reveals our ineptitude so He can get us out of the way. We advertise our credentials so others can be sure of us; He lets our assets fail us so others see that apart from God we can do nothing.

Conventional wisdom contends that weakness is a hindrance. We must be strong and able. But in spiritual matters, flaws and frailties are valuable leadership traits. For one thing they help others count less on our leadership and make them more dependent on God to find their way.

Moses is a good example of this notion. His experience, his background, his talents, his training had earned him the admiration of God's people. They looked to Moses for their deliverance. Yet they soon learned that all such hope was vain, that their leader, at best, was as weak and frail as they. He could not break through Pharaoh's defenses; he could not reduce Israel's servitude; he could not set his people free. And thus the way was prepared for Israel to lean on God.

We are inclined to fix on personalities, to be impressed by intellect, education, leadership skills, the passion of a leader's causes or strength of will. We believe that wisdom and power are vested in that person. Such adulation, however, is nothing more than humanism—making man or woman the measure of all things. What's worse, it's idolatry: a false centering on someone other than God.

And so God lets our leaders fall off their pedestals. Failure, indecision, and inability to achieve what they've set out to do bring humbling certainty of their inadequacy and strip their followers of illusion and their dependency. Such weaknesses show us that they, as do we, "shuffle along on feet of clay," to use Brennan Manning's phrase. They teach us that the only good thing about us, whatever our position, is the goodness of God.

Our Lord knew this truth well. He was fully aware that anything good in Him came not from Himself but from His Father. When an effusive disciple began to gush, "Good teacher . . ." Jesus stopped him in his tracks. "Why do you call me good?" He said. "No one is good—except God" (Mark 10:18).[7] ❧

Jannes and Jambres

The power of Sauron is still less than fear makes it.
—J. R. R. TOLKIEN

WARM-UP: *Exodus 7:11–12, 22*

*J*annes and Jambres were the two court magicians who opposed Moses and Aaron before Pharaoh. They're unnamed in the Old Testament, but in his second letter to Timothy, Paul uses the names tradition has assigned them (2 Timothy 3:8).

The two men appear frequently in extra-biblical sources as dark wizards. According to Jewish tradition, it was they who led Egypt's pharaoh astray until he and his army met death in the sea, where the two magicians perished as well. One ancient traveler, Macarius of Alexandria, claimed he visited their garden tomb in Upper Egypt, an immense monument dedicated to the memory of their immense power and influence.

The essence of all the traditions regarding these magicians is their deliberate and determined opposition to God, driven by the forces of evil. One of the Dead Sea Scrolls relates how Moses and Aaron arose with the help of the Prince of Lights, while Belial (Satan) raised up Yohanah (Jannes) and his brother. For this reason many believe that Jannes and Jambres are the source of the German legend of Johann Faust, the magician and alchemist who sold his soul to the devil in exchange for power and knowledge.

But the biblical record is sparse. It simply reports that Jannes and Jambres were Pharoah's magicians who through their magic were able to duplicate the plague on the Nile. They were also able to counterfeit the plague of frogs, but were unable to remove it, which suggests that the devil and his minions have no power to alleviate human suffering. It is our God of mercy who brings eternal consolation.

The magicians were frustrated at last by the plague of lice and confessed that their powers were limited. This is "the finger of God," they said, in that this stroke could not be explained by natural causes. In the end, they were overwhelmed by the plague of boils and driven from Pharaoh's court in disgrace (Exodus 9:11).

Paul, in speaking of the opponents of the Gospel in his day, says of them: "Just as Jannes and Jambres opposed Moses, so these men also oppose the truth, men of depraved mind, rejected as regards the faith. But they will not make further progress; for their folly will be obvious to all, as also that of those two [Jannes and Jambres] came to be" (2 Timothy 3:8–9 NASB).

Interesting word, *folly*. Paul's term means "to lack understanding." Those who promote error don't "get it." They may have a modicum of knowledge, but they have no real understanding, no answers for the deep distress of human existence, no counsel for the issues that break our hearts, which is why, in the end, even their own people turn away from them.

Furthermore, Paul says, they are wicked—"men of depraved mind" to use his precise phrase. Under the surface lies darkness and moral corruption. Though suave on the surface, they are rotten to the core, and their character will come to the surface in time and be seen by all.

The only people who are seduced into cults and ensconced in them are those who want to be. In time, those who truly want God will always see through such deception. "The Lord knows those who are his," Paul assures us, and He will not let His children go (2 Timothy 2:19).

And so we need not fear those who inveigh against the truth, though we feel their presence and though they grow in strength and numbers. In due time, their folly and impotence will be manifest.

"Every plant that my heavenly Father has not planted will be pulled up by the roots," Jesus said. "Leave them [alone]" (Matthew 15:13–14). ❧

Less of Us

A little more of God will make up for
a good deal less of you.
—GEORGE MACDONALD

WARM-UP: *Exodus 18:13–23*

The people of Israel were camped in the desert near the "mountain of God." It was a day of rest and the cloud remained stationary, spreading itself out as a canopy, protecting Israel from the heat of the sun.

On that day Moses seated himself to meet with his people—as he did every day that Israel was at rest—and the people queued up to seek his counsel. They stood in line and waited "from morning till evening." Everyone who had a marital or parental problem, a sin issue, some confusion or doubt, came to Moses to "inquire of God."

But the load was too great: too many people, too many problems, too many pressing needs. Moses could not continue to work all day, every day, without wearing out body and soul.

Jethro, the aged priest of Midian and Moses' father-in-law, saw the problem and warned his son-in-law. Moses had not yet felt the strain. He was fresh and full of enthusiasm for the work. But it was sapping his strength, and Jethro knew it. In later years, as Moses aged, he would know it as well. In time he would break down under the load (Numbers 11:10–15).

We don't always see the cost of our work, especially when we're young and full of enthusiasm. We're sustained by the excitement, the potential, the rush, the opportunities to be seized at the cost of a little more time and effort. These conceal the expenditure of our reserves. It's an act of love when some Jethro comes to warn us.

It cannot be God's will for us to wear ourselves out. He knows us too well to overtax us and drive us beyond human endurance. The burden He gives may be heavy, but if it's *His* burden it cannot be too heavy. It's *our* work—the work we add to His—that wears us out.

Jethro's advice was timely, for it spelled out for Moses (and for us) the work God intends for us to do. "Listen now to me," Jethro said, "and I will give you some advice, and may God be with you. *You must be the people's representative before God* and bring their disputes to him. *Teach them the decrees and laws,* and show them the way to live and the duties they are to perform. But *select capable men from all the people*—men who fear God, trustworthy men who hate dishonest gain—and appoint them as officials over thousands, hundreds, fifties and tens" (Exodus 18:19–21, italics added).

Moses' work was threefold: to pray, to teach, and to equip others for the work of the ministry. "If you do this and God so commands," Jethro said, "you will be able to stand the strain, and all these people will go home satisfied" (Exodus 18:23).

"Is there not a thought here for the Lord's workers?" F. B. Meyer asks. "Are we not dissipating our energies over too wide an area? Are we not embracing in our life many things that others could do better? Ought not those who are gifted with the power of prayer and spiritual insight to cultivate those sides of their nature, leaving the details of management and the direction of finances to others? We should live on the greatest side of our nature, reserving ourselves for that—not careless of minor details, if there is no one else to manage them, but prepared to hand them over to 'able men and women,' even though they may have to learn their duties at a cost, in the beginning, of some mistakes and failures . . . .

"We touch others most when we most touch God. The prophet and priest, the teacher, these are among the choicest gifts of God. And if you are gifted specially in these directions, culti-vate such endowments to the uttermost—they are rare enough—leaving other details to be cared for by others who may be cast in a more practical mould."

This was the wisdom and strength of the early church. As it grew in numbers and more of the apostles' time was demanded, the Twelve enlisted the help of other gifted individuals to address the physical needs of the church while they gave themselves "to prayer and the ministry of the word." Thus, said Luke, "the word of God spread" and "the number of disciples in Jerusalem increased rapidly" (Acts 6:1–7).

"Is there not a thought here for the Lord's workers?" F. B. Meyer would ask. ❦

The Place of Rest

With [God's] left hand he governs the world through the ordinances of the world. And now he has suddenly removed his left hand, and we are committed with an unparalleled immediacy and exclusiveness to God's right hand. Now we have to reach out for this right hand of God and let it be the pillow on which we rest, the watcher at our bed, the guide on our dark and uncertain path, and our staff in the valley of the shadow.

—Martin Luther

WARM-UP: *Exodus 33:1–16*

*M*oses was leaving the slopes of Horeb and venturing into uncharted territory, moving from the known to the unknown. He had no idea what he would encounter in the wilderness. He only knew that a vast, untracked, and terrible desert lay ahead, inhabited by militant and merciless foes. The future seemed dark and foreboding—as do *our* days of uncertainty. "What was, may be less dark than what is to be," Tolkien's wise Gandalf said to the hobbit Frodo.

Furthermore, God had distanced Himself from His people. His tent had been moved "outside the camp some distance away." And are there not days that we wonder if God has written us off in our sin?

Then there was Moses' loneliness. Though he lived among millions, Moses had no equals, no spiritual peers, no counselor wiser than he, no one to whom he could unburden his heart and be understood. He bore alone, on his shoulders, the burden of his people, like Atlas carrying the world.

In these circumstances God gave Moses this bold assurance: "My Presence will go with you, and I will give you rest" (Exodus 33:14).

Note well the place where that assurance was given: in the tent that Moses pitched for God outside the camp, the "tent of meeting." This is the place where "the LORD would speak to Moses face to face, as a man speaks with his friend" (Exodus 33:11). Here Moses found counsel for the peril of his day. Here an amazing dialogue took place.

Moses reminded God of past assurances: "You have said, 'I know you by name and you have found favor with me.'" Thus his great heart was emboldened to ask for more. "If you are pleased with me, teach me your ways so I may know you and continue to find favor with you." Or put another way: "Will *you* be my counselor and companion?" And God replied readily, "My Presence will go with you, and I will give you rest" (Exodus 33:12–14).

The second person pronouns are singular. "My presence will go with *you*, and I will give *you* rest [peace]." God did not promise, at least on this occasion, that He would accompany Israel on her journey or that she would reach her destination. Nor did He promise Moses that he would enjoy a carefree life of affluence and ease. He only promised to be with His servant and make Him a center of peace in the midst of the confusion and uncertainty of his day.

God will do the same for you. He does not promise that you will enjoy a tranquil, trouble-free existence or that you will be carried to heaven "in flowery beds of ease." But He does utter the simple promise: "My presence will go with *you*, and I will give *you* rest."

God hath not promised skies always blue,
Flower-strewn pathways all our lives thro';
God hath not promised sun without rain,
Joy without sorrow, peace without pain.

But God hath promised strength for the day,
Rest for the labor, light for the way,
Grace for the trials, help from above,
Unfailing sympathy, undying love.

God hath not promised, we shall not know
Toil and temptation, trouble and woe;
He hath not told us we shall not bear
Many a burden, many a care.

But God hath promised strength for the day,
Rest for the labor, light for the way,
Grace for the trials, help from above,
Unfailing sympathy, undying love.

God hath not promised smooth roads and wide,
Swift, easy travel, needing no guide;
Never a mountain, rocky and steep,
Never a river turbid and deep.

But God hath promised strength for the day,
Rest for the labor, light for the way,
Grace for the trials, help from above,
Unfailing sympathy, undying love.

— Annie Johnson Flint

Eldad and Medad

There's no end of the good you can do if
you don't care who gets the credit for it.
—COACH JOHN WOODEN

WARM-UP: *Numbers 11:16–29*

*M*oses lamented: "I cannot carry all these people by myself; the burden is too heavy for me." God, who fully understood Moses' weariness, gathered Israel before the tabernacle. There, He took some of the Spirit that was on Moses and put that Spirit on seventy of the elders of Israel (Numbers 11:14, 16–17). Each worker was filled and flooded with the fullness of the invisible God.

Then the Spirit broke forth. Sixty-eight of the seventy elders prophesied for a time and then ceased. But two continued to prophesy.

A young man ran and told Moses, "Eldad and Medad are prophesying in the camp!" And Joshua, equally jealous for Moses' honor, added his sentiment: "Moses, my lord, stop them!"

"Are you jealous for my sake?" Moses replied. "I wish that all the LORD's people were prophets and that the LORD would put his Spirit on them!"

This one remark establishes the greatness of Moses.

Little souls are addicted to their own significance. They're annoyed when others gain prominence, for they, like Diotrophes, "love to be first" (3 John 9). They seek greatness for themselves, though in time this always has the opposite effect. In Dante's "Inferno," the poet's vision of hell, he portrays those who have esteemed themselves more highly than others carrying boulders on their shoulders that bend them double so they can only look at the ground, for on earth they always looked down on others.

Those who exhibit enduring greatness delight in seeing others use their gifts; they are content to decrease if others increase. They serve the glory of Christ, and the good of His people. They have no greater joy than to hear that their children walk in truth and are surpassing them.

There is no more searching test than this: Am I as eager for God's kingdom to come through others as I am for it to come through me?

I ask myself: Do I take joy in the success of others, even my "competition" (Philippians 1:18)? Can I pray for and encourage younger, more gifted men and women who take my place? Can I esteem them more highly than I do myself (Philippians 2:3)? Am I willing to be anything (or nothing) if God's eternal purposes are served?

I cannot ask these questions without feeling shame, for they expose the selfish ambition that is mingled with all other motives. Oh, that you and I could say with Moses, "I wish that *all* the LORD's people were prophets and that the LORD would put his Spirit on them," and rejoice in *their* joy when they're honored and exalted beyond us.

"Let us know how to sit, as well as how to rise," wrote John Wesley, "and let it comfort our declining days to trace, in those who are likely to succeed us in our work, the openings of yet greater usefulness."

This spirit can only grow in us as we are taken into God's great heart and see His passion to be glorified in *all* His saints (2 Thessalonians 1:10). There we learn to care more for H*is* work than for our own.

If I would do great things, John reminds me: "I must decrease" (John 3:30 NASB). ✺

Something Wicked

Something wicked this way comes.
—RAY BRADBURY

WARM-UP: *Numbers 25:1–3*

*B*alak was the ancient king of Moab who hired the wizard Balaam to curse Israel. Balaam couldn't curse the nation directly so he "taught Balak to entice the Israelites to sin by . . . committing sexual immorality" (Revelation 2:14).

Balaam is long gone, but his spirit endures to this day.

Balaam's spirit lies behind the efforts of movie and television producers, magazine and book publishers, and other media people to push their prurience on us. They claim it's a matter of art and freedom of expression, but I'm convinced it's something more.

Some would say it is simple greed. Running scared by their need for sales and ratings, media moguls are driven mad by the smell of our money. They know the public is tired of the trite and banal material coming from the media and are looking elsewhere for their entertainment.[8] So instead of producing something of merit, they have resorted to the time-honored tradition of stimulating our libido—using skin to lure us in. Sad to say, it works.

But it does go beyond greed. Otherwise, why would these people be so compulsive about their prurience and so hostile toward traditional notions of family life, marriage, human sexuality, and public decency? And why do they denigrate and so savagely satirize those who advocate another, saner morality? What's bugging them?

No, it's more than just trying to assure us that the old ways are obsolete so they can sell us more of their stuff. There is another,

31

more perverse market strategy at work here. Someone is trying to sell us down the river.

Long ago, Solomon, the wisest man on earth, observed that cheap sex costs too much: it robs us of strength and dignity as men and women and reduces us to ruin. "You give your best strength to others and your years to one who is cruel.... At the end of your life you will groan, when your flesh and body are spent" (Proverbs 5:9–11).

It occurs to me, then, that if there were some plot to subvert us and make us less than we are intended to be—God's most glorious creation—the best way to go about that subversion would be to convince us that pornography, marital infidelity, and other sexual perversities are nothing more than high-jinks and good clean fun. And the best way to drum that deception into our heads would be to portray it onscreen, onstage, or on the page, where the lines between fantasy and reality can be so easily erased. Fantasy evil can be made to look like nothing more than a healthy frolic while fantasy good can look exceedingly dull.

But fantasy isn't reality, and nothing good ever comes from the random couplings I'm aware of. There's no romance, no intimacy, no loving or lasting relationships in them, and in the end the people involved are ruined. What sensual enjoyment remains is nothing more than an effort to find refuge from one's misery.

And then there are those cruel eventualities that result from efforts to find relief from the emptiness and guilt in alcohol, drugs, and other mind-numbing pharmaceuticals—and the inevitable inclination to increase the dose. And for an increasing number of people, there is the terrible finality of AIDS.

No, there's more going on here than simple greed. "Something wicked this way comes." Some diabolical fiend is hatching a plot to steal our souls.

Oh, media people may not consciously be malicious; they're only mercenary. But, like Balak, they've become unwitting agents of the one whom Jesus said has been a liar and a murderer from the beginning (John 8:44), whose strategy has always been to deceive, and whose eternal objective is to destroy, to blight and ruin and make us less than God wants us to be.

Yes, there are venal people out there scheming to take away our money. But more importantly, there's a cold-blooded killer out there lusting for our souls. I don't think we ought to fall for any of it. ❦

A Time for Intolerance

"When I use a word," Humpty Dumpty said in a scornful tone, "it means just what I choose it to mean—neither more nor less."

"The question is," said Alice, "whether you can make words mean so many different things."

—LEWIS CARROLL

WARM-UP: *Numbers 25*

*I*srael first came in contact with the fertility cults of Canaan at Shittim where certain Israelite men "began to indulge in sexual immorality with Moabite women." Before long, these women had encouraged the men to sacrifice to their gods, and the ultimate consequence was that "Israel joined in worshiping Baal."

According to later Scriptures, this seduction came at the suggestion of Balaam, the wizard "who taught Balak to entice the Israelites to sin by eating food sacrificed to idols and by committing sexual immorality" (Revelation 2:14). Balaam couldn't curse Israel so he used sex to lure them away from obedience to God.

In the midst of God's anger and the people's repentance, "an Israelite man brought to his family a Midianite woman right before the eyes of Moses and the whole assembly of Israel while they were weeping [in repentance] at the entrance to the Tent of Meeting." He took the woman into the Holy of Holies and "lay" with her there, before the Ark of God. (The word "tent" in 25:8 refers to the inner sanctuary of the tabernacle.)[9]

Jerome, in his translation of this text, uses the Latin word *lupanar* (brothel) to stress the fact that the Holy of Holies—the holiest place in the universe—was desecrated.

The scene is shocking, or at least it ought to be. But sad to say, scenes equally shocking play out in our own culture, where anything and everything goes and we're expected to tolerate it.

But when Phinehas, a grandson of Aaron, saw what was happening, he strode into the tabernacle and, filled with God's Spirit and in holy outrage, quickly dispatched the two of them. ("It's not for nothing," J. B. Phillips said, "that the Spirit God has given to us is called the *Holy* Spirit.")

This is not an act we're called upon to duplicate these days, but it is a clear instance when *intolerance* was a perfectly good and useful idea.

Fifteen hundred years ago Augustine pointed out that the best way to undercut an opponent's argument is to co-opt his language: take his words, assign them new meanings, and make them your own. That way your opponent has to stop and define his terms, or invent new ones. Either way, his arguments lose force.

"Intolerance" is one of those words that have been co-opted and given a new set of meanings by God's opponents. Today, intolerance has become the worst sin in the world's eyes and tolerance the highest good. To be principled or to have informed moral convictions is to be declared intolerant, out of touch, and, above all, mean-spirited. The "tolerant," those who tolerate anything and everything, thus take the moral high ground.

G. K. Chesterton once said that morality, like art, consists of drawing a very fine line. Now, it seems to me, we can't draw any lines at all!

Whatever happened to moral judgment? Whatever happened to sin? ❦

What Does a Woman Want?

No people ever rise higher than the point
to which they elevate their women.
—ISABELLA THOBURN,
MISSIONARY TO INDIA (1840–1901)

WARM-UP: *Numbers 27:1–7; Joshua 17:3–4*

Zelophehad had five daughters—Mahlah, Noah, Hoglah, Milcah, and Tirzah—but no sons. According to the law of hereditary possession in the ancient Semitic world, a man's property passed solely to his sons or to the male members of the clan. Thus, when Zelophehad died, his five daughters could not inherit his land.

They came, however, and "stood before Moses, Eleazar the priest, the leaders and the whole assembly," and asked for their father's portion in the land. (Note that their request came before Israel had even gained possession of the Promised Land. These women, unlike the generation that perished in the wilderness, took God at His word!)

Moses took the matter before the Lord and the Lord took up the women's cause: "What Zelophehad's daughters are saying is right. You must certainly give them property as an inheritance among their father's relatives and turn their father's inheritance over to them."

Twenty-five years later, when the land was in Israel's hands, the daughters of Zelophehad appeared again before Eleazar the priest and the leaders of Israel, this time under the command of Joshua. "The LORD commanded Moses to give us an inheritance among our brothers," they said. So these good men, acting against the convention and bias of their day, but in obedience to God, "gave them an inheritance along with the brothers of their father, according to the LORD's command" (Joshua 17:4).

Hurrah for these men, and hurrah for the man who has the wisdom to set aside the prejudices of his day and give women their God-given inheritance. For, as Peter said, they are "heirs with you [men] of the gracious gift of life" (1 Peter 3:7).

No man should ever demean or belittle a woman, at least no man who claims The Name. For if we follow in the footsteps of Jesus, we follow a man who "never nagged at [women], never flattered, or coaxed, or patronized them; who rebuked without querulousness and praised without condescension; who took their questions and arguments seriously; who had no axe to grind and no uneasy male dignity to defend. There is no act, no sermon, no parable in the whole Gospel that borrows its pungency from female perversity; nobody could possibly guess from the words and deeds of Jesus that there was anything 'funny' about a woman's nature" (Dorothy Sayers, *Are Women Human?*).

Women are heirs with me of the life of God, fully equal in their capacity to know God and to grow into the full stature of Christ. To think otherwise is unmanly and ungodly. ❧

The Messengers

We must bide our time . . . approving the
high and ultimate purpose.
— J. R. R. Tolkien

WARM-UP: *Joshua 2*

There are two words for prostitute in Semitic languages: one refers to a temple prostitute (*qudshu*—a "holy one"), the other to a "working girl." Rahab was the latter.

I can't be sure, of course, because the account is necessarily sparse, but it seems to me that like all those who sell their bodies and souls she must have lived in quiet despair—all used up and empty, just trying to get through the day, waiting for what she did not know, until the day two men showed up.[10]

"Joshua son of Nun secretly sent two spies from Shittim. 'Go, look over the land,' he said. . . . So they went and entered the house of a prostitute named Rahab and stayed there" (Joshua 2:1).

The two spies crept into the city of Jericho and by chance came to Rahab's establishment. Strange chance, I say, if chance it was.

Jericho's intelligence network was at work and someone reported the spies to the king of Jericho, who sent his soldiers to search Rahab's house. But when the king's men came calling, Rahab hid the spies and sent the king's men off on a wild goose chase.

Here's the interesting thing to me: The great Canaanite city of Jericho was named for the profane moon god *Yeriq*, and was noted for its corrupt sensuality, *yet in this unlikely place lived a woman who longed for the living God.*

And so it is today. Here and there, in the most unlikely places, exist men and women looking for that elusive "something more," and God will move heaven and earth to bring salvation to those solitary souls.

On the face of it, the spies were sent into Jericho to reconnoiter, but on their return they brought back no intelligence that aided Joshua in his siege, no word of easy access through the city water system or defensive weakness in the wall. The only report they brought was information Joshua had already received (see Joshua 1:2–3,11,13 and 2:24).

No, in reality the spies were "messengers," to use Joshua's exact word (Joshua 6:25 NASB), sent to bring salvation to Rahab.

And so it is that we may "happen" upon some man or woman living in quiet desperation but enduring with the expectation that someday someone will bring him or her salvation. "How will I know?" we ask. That's not our business. Our responsibility is to be available to God, ready and willing to be put to His intended purpose. He will do the rest. He will get us to the right place, the right person, at the right time, and give us the right things to say.

Some years ago Carolyn and I were on a flight home from Frankfurt, Germany. It was the first leg of a long flight to Seattle, then to Boise and home. It had been an exhausting week of ministry for both of us and we were weary. I dropped off to sleep as soon as the plane took off, but was soon awakened by a disturbance in the aisle.

The flight attendant and a passenger seated on Carolyn's left were arguing about the man's seat assignment. Somehow, he had been separated from his fiancée who was seated several rows behind us.

The man grew increasingly angry and argumentative until another passenger, seated beside the man's fiancée, offered to trade places. The swap was arranged, and Carolyn's new seatmate settled into his place, drew out a legal pad, and began to work on some project.

As it happened, there was a young French boy seated on the man's left who wanted to talk. The man, who was the soul of patience, gave up his project after a few minutes and began to chat amiably with the garrulous child. Carolyn was soon drawn into the conversation.

I heard the man say he was from Los Gatos, California, a town close to Los Altos, where Carolyn and I had lived for eighteen years. He was on his way to San Francisco. I heard Carolyn remark on the fact that we had many friends in the Bay Area and then I went back to sleep.

When I awakened an hour later, I found Carolyn sharing her faith with her new friend, scribbling on his pad of paper, drawing diagrams, illustrating the Gospel. He was listening intently and asking questions. I sat there quietly and prayed for her and the man.

At one point he said, "You believe as my wife does."

"Oh?" Carolyn replied. "And how did she become a Christian?"

"Through Bible Study Fellowship," he responded.

"How did she learn about Bible Study Fellowship?" Carolyn asked.

"A friend of hers, Nell King, invited her to attend."

"That's remarkable!" Carolyn exclaimed. "Nell is one of my best friends!"

And then the coin dropped. Some months before we moved to Boise, Nell had asked Carolyn to pray for a friend who had become a Christian through Bible Study Fellowship and for her husband who was not yet a believer—*the man now seated on Carolyn's left*, there "by that power which erring men call chance," as Spenser said.

"The world is dying without Christ!" I say. "I must be busy!"

"No," the Spirit says. "You must be ready." 🌿

Double Trouble

No man is an island, entire of itself; every man
is a piece of the continent, a part of the main.
—JOHN DONNE (1572–1631)

WARM-UP: *Joshua 7*

A few days after the fall of Jericho, Joshua sent a small contingent of 3,000 men to lay siege to the city of Ai, the next enemy enclave targeted for capture. The *NIV Study Bible* notes that an advance to Ai "would bring Israel beyond the Jordan Valley and provide them a foothold in the central highlands."

Ai had once been a strategic stronghold. Artifacts from an earlier period suggest it was occupied by the Egyptians for a number of years and was the city from which they ruled Canaan, but it had been destroyed shortly before Israel's invasion. Now it was only a heap of ruins defended by a small outpost of Canaanites. (The name *Ai* actually means "ruins.") Ai was a pushover, a piece of cake. UCLA *vs.* Slippery Rock.

But the siege became a debacle. Ai's little army "chased the Israelites from the city gate as far as the stone quarries and struck them down on the slopes" (Joshua 7:5). Israel was routed and pushed back to the Jordan, losing the ground they had gained at Jericho and suffering the first and only casualties of the campaign: thirty-two fine young men fell before the counterattack. Ai was the mouse that roared.

The defeat was an ominous sign, and "the hearts of the people [the Israelites] melted and became like water." What if their enemies now formed a coalition against them? They regrouped to lick their wounds and grieve over their dead while Joshua determined to find out what had gone wrong.

Joshua tore his clothes and fell facedown to the ground before the ark of the LORD, remaining there till evening. The elders of Israel did the same, and sprinkled dust on their heads. And Joshua said, "Ah, Sovereign LORD, why did you ever bring this people across the Jordan to deliver us into the hands of the Amorites to destroy us? If only we had been content to stay on the other side of the Jordan! O LORD, what can I say, now that Israel has been routed by its enemies? The Canaanites and the other people of the country will hear about this and they will surround us and wipe out our name from the earth. What then will you do for your own great name?" (Joshua 7:6–9).

Joshua's anxiety and perplexity falls short of the calm confidence of Moses, but he was still a young leader and his faith needed time to grow. He struggled with his confusion and doubt and then exclaimed, in so many words, "What are you going to do about this, Lord?"

The Lord replied, "Israel has sinned; they have violated my covenant, which I commanded them to keep. They have taken some of the devoted things; they have stolen, they have lied, they have put them with their own possessions" (Joshua 7:10-11).

God put His finger squarely on the trouble: Someone had taken objects from Jericho that were "devoted" (Joshua 7:1); that is, they were articles that were to be set apart for the Lord or were to be destroyed.

Before the siege of Jericho, Joshua had warned Israel, "The city and all that is in it are to be devoted to the LORD. . . . Keep away from the devoted things, so that you will not bring about your own destruction by taking any of them. Otherwise you will make the camp of Israel liable to destruction and bring trouble on it" (Joshua 6:17-18).

Exactly what was to be destroyed and why, we aren't told, but my best guess is that there was something especially corrupting about Jericho. The inhabitants of that place were devotees of the moon god *Yerig*, for whom the city was named, and were perhaps evangelistic in their zeal for that religion. One early Christian, Saint Isidore of Seville, considered Jericho to be the fountainhead of the "heretical teachings" of the Canaanites that would surely contaminate God's people.

Moon worship had an attractive and seductive pull, yet it was degrading (like cyber-porn). God wanted Israel to stay away from everything associated with this pagan religion because He knew that even slight contact would corrupt and "bring trouble" on them.

You can read the rest of the story yourself. It's enough to say that one man, "Achan son of Carmi, the son of Zimri, the son of Zerah, of the tribe of Judah . . . acted unfaithfully in regard to the devoted things" (Joshua 7:1). One man plundered Jericho, hid his small treasure, and plunged the entire nation into ruin.

Achan was double trouble, as his name suggests.[11] He troubled himself and he troubled others. Though he acted alone, "he was not the only one who died for his sin" (Joshua 22:20). He brought death and destruction to his family and friends.

That's the trouble with sin, you see. You cannot contain it. In time it will destroy you and all that you love.

The writer of Hebrews warns us: "See to it that . . . no bitter root grows up to cause trouble and defile many" (Hebrews 12:15). This metaphor—a "bitter [lethal] root"—is drawn from the words of Moses: "Make sure there is no man or woman, clan or tribe among you today whose heart turns away from the LORD our God . . . make sure there is no root among you that produces such bitter poison" (Deuteronomy 29:18).

The bitter root is a heart that has turned away from the Lord. Like a poisonous plant that finds its way into a family meal, it imperils everyone at the table. Our transgressions can bring death and destruction to our household.

May there be no root in us that produces such lethal fruit. ❧

If I Had a Hammer

If I had a hammer, I'd hammer in the morning,
I'd hammer in the evening, all over this land.
—PETE SEEGER

WARM-UP: *Judges 4:17–24*

*D*orothy Sayers claimed that Sigmund Freud's question, "What does a woman want?" is frivolous. "What is unreasonable and irritating is to assume that all one's tastes and preferences have to be conditioned by the class to which one belongs."

For her, the appropriate question is not, "What do women want?" but rather, what does *this* woman want? "Are all women created to do the same thing?" she asked. "The obvious answer is no, of course not. Never in the course of history and least of all now. Men and women are created to do a special thing in the world. Their task is to find that thing."

Which brings me to the story of Jael and the "special thing" she was created to do.

In the days of the judges, Sisera was the commander of the Canaanite army. His army was heavily armed with nine hundred iron chariots. But God gave the Israelites the victory. "All the troops of Sisera fell by the sword; not a man was left"—except Sisera, who fled on foot north toward Hazor, his command post. He had almost reached safety when he came upon a Kenite camp.

Sisera had every reason to expect sanctuary with the Kenites. They were a friendly tribe that honored the ancient rules and conventions of hospitality in that part of the world. So Sisera fled to the tent of Heber, the head of the tribe. There he was welcomed by Jael, Heber's wife.

The writer describes the scene in detail: Jael invites Sisera in and, when he tells her he is thirsty, gives him "thickened milk," a yogurt drink that was mildly soporific. She then hides him under a blanket, where the thoroughly frightened and exhausted man drops off to sleep—a sleep from which he never awakens.

While he slumbers, Jael takes a tent peg and the mallet with which the pegs were driven into the ground and hammers the stake through Sisera's head!

Soon, Barak, the Israeli commander who is pursuing Sisera, comes by the camp. Jael goes out to meet him and leads him to her tent, lifts the flap, and shows him the gory sight.

As Deborah, the judge and prophetess had predicted, the honor of the victory was not Barak's, for the Lord had delivered Sisera into a *woman's* hands (Judges 4:9).

On that day, Deborah sang a song commemorating Jael's deed:

Her hand reached for the tent peg,
  her right hand for the workman's hammer.
She struck Sisera, she crushed his head,
  she shattered and pierced his temple. (5:26)

In those words, you can hear the lethal hammer blows! Jael, the Terminator!

There's something terrible and grand about this woman: terrible because we wince at her bloody act; grand because we witness her zeal for God. Jael's savage sledge was a hammer of justice, and from that day on "the hand of the Israelites grew stronger and stronger against Jabin, the Canaanite king, until they destroyed him" (4:24). Her heroic act was the beginning of the end of Canaanite control, and thus Israel, the repository of the "seed" of our salvation, was spared.

"Most blessed of women be Jael," Deborah sang, a phrase reminiscent of Elizabeth's blessing of Mary, the mother of Jesus.

And what did Jael do to merit such praise? She did the thing she was created to do.

Admittedly, not many women (or men, for that matter) are called to carry out such violent acts. Most of our obedience comes in the ordinary affairs of everyday life. But we never know what heroism lies in quiet obedience to God, and there's no biblical reason why a woman, in her obedience, may not play an extraordinary role in the unfolding drama of world redemption.

Carlo Carretto, the twentieth century Italian theologian and mystic, writes:

> Today, a woman must hear the words of Jesus as a man hears them; and if Jesus says, "Go and make disciples of all nations," it must no longer be that a man hears this in one way and a woman in another.
>
> How you must re-think everything! And how I would like to say to women of today, "Go!" with all the force of which my spirit is capable, and all my anxiety for the immense needs of a world athirst for the Gospel. This is an urgent invitation. Let your toil, wherever it is, be illumined by the power of your calling—for you were made to serve.
>
> Do not copy men. Be authentic. Seek, in your femaleness, the root that distinguishes you from them. It is unmistakable, for it has been willed and created by God himself. Repeat to yourselves every day: A man is not a woman.
>
> —from Carretto's *I Francis*

Women are fully equal to men in their capacity to know God, to learn from Him, and to do what He calls them to do. So (and here I speak to women), seek in your created role as a woman the "root that distinguishes you" and follow Jesus. You cannot imagine where He will take you and what He will do with you there, but I can tell you this: He is "able to do immeasurably more than all [you] ask or imagine, according to his power that is at work within [you]" (Ephesians 3:20).

I say then to us men, when we belittle women and minimize their abilities, when we attempt to curb their God-given gifts and creativity and restrict their service, when we think that women, merely because they are women, will reason irrationally, act irresponsibly, or fold under pressure, we've missed what is said again and again in God's Word. There is "neither . . . male nor female" (Galatians 3:28). When it comes to doing God's will, the differences between men and women—whatever they are—make no difference at all. ❧

Payday Someday

This is a court of law, young man,
not a court of justice.
—OLIVER WENDELL HOLMES
TO ONE OF HIS CLERKS

WARM-UP: *Judges 9*

*A*bimelech was Gideon's son by a Canaanite woman. After his father's death, he went to his mother's clan and proposed that they support him in his political ambitions. "Which is better for you," he asked. "To have all seventy of Jerub-Baal's sons rule over you, or just one man? Remember, I am your flesh and blood." His mother's brothers agreed to his plan and took the matter to the elders of Shechem, who gave the aspiring young man seventy pieces of silver from the treasury of Baal to finance his campaign.

Unfortunately, Abimelech was an opportunist, driven by selfish ambition and a jealous hatred of his brothers. His first act of "leadership" was to hire a bunch of thugs to eliminate the competition. Abimelech and his gorillas assassinated his brothers, one at a time, on a stone in ritual sacrifice. Only Jotham, the youngest son of Gideon, escaped.

The bloody deed accomplished, "all the citizens of Shechem and Beth Millo gathered beside the great tree at the pillar in Shechem to crown Abimelech king."

From the mountain of Gerezim, the Mount of Blessings, which rose above the valley, Jotham, the last survivor of the bloody massacre of Gideon's house, watched the proceedings. When the coronation ceremony was over, he began to shout out a parable— a story about a kingdom of trees that were about to elect a king.

The kingdom of trees asked an olive tree, a fig tree, and then a grape vine to rule, but each in turn refused, for none was willing to "flutter" over the trees, as the Hebrew text puts it, an idiom suggesting trivial, wasted effort. All the other trees declined as well, until the only tree left was the bramble, which bore no fruit, offered no shade, and was a menace to those who tried to control it. (Brambles not only spread rapidly and render the ground useless, but also become dangerous fire hazards during the heat of summer.)

The parable was apt, for after three years of Abimelech's petty tyranny (as the word "governed" in 9:22 implies), the people of Shechem had had enough. They hired bandits to wait on the mountain passes that surrounded Abimelech's kingdom and ambush caravans passing along the trade routes to deprive him of necessary revenue.

Next they cast their lot with a newcomer to the area named Gaal, who bragged, "if the people were under my command, I would get rid of Abimelech." (The plot is reminiscent of any number of Wild West movies, with a tough, young, fast-draw artist trying to make a name for himself, shooting off his mouth after having too much to drink in a local saloon.)

But Abimelech called Gaal's bluff and eventually ran him and his hooligans out of town.

Abimelech, in retaliation for Shechem's conspiracy, slaughtered the inhabitants as they were working in their fields, razed the city and sowed it with salt to make the land infertile. The people who escaped fled to nearby Beth Millo, where they took sanctuary in a stone tower. Abimelech had his men gather green branches, pile them around the base of the tower and set them on fire, asphyxiating those who had taken sanctuary there.

But even this bloodbath did not satisfy Abimelech. Now paranoid and utterly out of control, he began to destroy the rest of his kingdom, turning his rage on another of his towns, the city of Thebez. Its inhabitants fled to their tower and were about to suffer the fate of those at Beth Millo when some unnamed woman dropped an "upper millstone"—a rock about the size of a Frisbee but weighing a good deal more—on Abimelech's head and "cracked his skull."

Shamed that it was a woman who had done him in, and unwilling to die at her hands, Abimelech ordered his armor bearer to finish the job with his sword, which the young man seemed only too happy to do (9:54). *Sic transit gloria.*

Was all this an accident of history? No, "God did this," Israel's historian assures us. "Thus God repaid the wickedness that Abimelech had done" (Judges 9:56).

We see cruel tyrants everywhere getting away with appalling evil, and we wonder if anyone is minding the store. That's because we see only one side of God—His tender mercy and longsuffering patience. He waits, not willing that any should perish. But His tolerance is not the whole story.

Psalm 73 makes the same point. The poet was having a hard time with God, who allowed evil men and women to run amok in His world (Psalm 73:1–12). He struggled with God's injustice until he entered the sanctuary, the place of revelation. There he saw the "final destiny" of the wicked.

"Surely you place them on slippery ground;
  you cast them down to ruin.
How suddenly are they destroyed,
  completely swept away by terrors!
As a dream when one awakes,
  so when you arise, O Lord,
  you will despise them as fantasies" (Psalm 73:18–20).

Evil men and women are on a slippery slope to the grave. There, they will be swept away and "cast down to ruin."

"Man is destined to die once, and after that to face judgment" (Hebrews 9:27). All things considered, it's a very fair world. ❧

A Wandering One

They felt good eyes upon them
and shrunk within—undone;
good parents had good children
and they—a wandering one.
—RUTH BELL GRAHAM

WARM-UP: *Judges 13:2–21*

*M*anoah prayed to the Lord: "Teach us how to bring up the boy who is to be born" (Judges 13:8). This is the earnest and often anxious prayer of every godly parent.

The boy was Samson, Israel's prankish Hercules, who squandered his God-given strength. One wonders how often Manoah and his wife awakened in the dark, sleepless hours of the night and asked themselves, "Where did we go wrong?"

When our children make bad choices—when they abuse alcohol, do drugs, get pregnant out of wedlock, drop out of school, turn their backs on God and family—we ask ourselves the same question. We blame ourselves and see our children as the tragic victims of our ineptitude.

There is, however, no absolute correlation between the ways we parent and the way our children turn out. Good parenting makes a difference, but it does not *guarantee* that the product of that parenting will be good.

We all are acquainted with families where neglect, violence, and substance abuse are the norm, yet the children turn out remarkably well. They have good friends; they do well in school; they hold good jobs; they end up in stable marriages, and they handle their own parental responsibilities with wisdom and love.

And we all are familiar with families where the parents are warm, nurturing, kind, firm, wise, and giving—and yet there's at least one prodigal in the family and sometimes more than one.

Despite our best efforts, our children may go wrong.

But, you say, what about the proverb: "Train a child in the way he should go, and when he is old he will not turn from it" (Proverbs 22:6)? That sounds very much like a guarantee.

We must remember, however, that the biblical proverbs are not promises, but *premises*—general rules or axioms. Proverbs 22:6 is a statement of general truth, much like our contemporary saying: "As the twig is bent so the tree is inclined." A proverb is a saying that sets forth a truth that is applicable in most cases, but there are always exceptions to the rule.

Why these exceptions? Because children are not mindless matter that we can shape at will. They are autonomous individuals who may, with the best of parenting, choose to go their own way. Even God, the perfect parent, has always had trouble with His children— Adam and Eve to name two. (You and me to name two more.)

If we believe that by applying certain techniques and rules we can secure godly behavior in our children, we may be in for bitter disillusionment and heartache. No one can determine nor can they predict what their offspring will do.

It was Joaquin Andujar, poet and pitcher for the St. Louis Cardinals, who said you can sum up baseball in one word: "You never know." His word count was off, but he captured the essence of life as well as baseball.

Given that uncertainty, the question is not "How can I produce godly children?" but rather, "How can I be a godly parent?" The two questions may appear to be the same, but they're not. The first has to do with result, over which we have no control; the second with process, over which we do, by God's grace, have some measure of control.

If our focus is on process, then the questions are about us: How can I deal with my impatience, temper and rage, my selfishness, my resentment, my stubbornness, my defensiveness, my pride, my laziness, my unwillingness to listen? How can I deal with my addictions? How can I strengthen my marriage? How can I develop my parenting skills? How can I build bridges of grace, forgiveness, and acceptance that will make it possible for my prodigal to come home?

These are the matters that must occupy us as parents ... and then we must leave the results with God.[12]

Ruth Bell Graham expresses it well:

Lord, I will straighten all I can and You
take over what we mothers cannot do. ❦

Godliman Street

It is better to be silent and to be.
—FROM A LETTER TO THE EPHESIANS
BY IGNATIUS (C. A.D. 110)

WARM-UP: *1 Samuel 9:3–6*

*S*ome years ago my wife, Carolyn, and I were walking through the streets of London, making our way toward Saint Paul's Cathedral, when we noticed a street named "Godliman." It was an insignificant little byway, not much longer than a football field, but the name stuck in my mind.

Later, after we had returned home, I learned from an old book written by a nineteenth-century Londoner that on that street had lived a gentleman whose life was so saintly that it became known as the street of the "godly man," which eventually evolved into Godliman Street. This etiology reminded me of a story from the days of early Israel.

It seems that Kish, the father of Saul, had lost his donkeys— a matter of some consequence in his day—and had sent his son and a servant to find the straying animals. From their home in Gibeah, the two young men traveled northeast some twenty miles, ascending the east slope of Mount Ephraim and passing down the other side. From there they turned to the northwest to the land of Shalishah, then south to Shaalim and into the borders of Benjamin's tribal allotment. Altogether they made a circuit of over a hundred miles, but caught no sight of the donkeys.

Thinking that their long absence might cause his father more worry than the missing animals, Saul suggested that he and the servant return home. But his servant pointed toward Ramah,

Samuel's village, and replied, "Look, in this town there is a man of God; he is highly respected, and everything he says comes true. Let's go there now. Perhaps he will tell us what way to take."

So Saul and his servant hastened to Ramah, where they found Samuel and explained their plight—and gained a good deal more than they expected (but that's another story; cf. 1 Samuel 10:1).

What intrigues me most about this tale is the reputation that Samuel had earned as "a man of God." The old prophet had retired from his work and was no longer in the public eye, yet the fragrance of his life lingered on. His presence was "weighty," to use an Old Testament idiom.

"He is highly respected," (1 Samuel 9:6) is the way the NIV translators render the verb *kabod*, in an effort to turn it into formal English, but the essential meaning of the Hebrew word is "heavy." It's the term used elsewhere in Samuel to describe Eli's corpulence: "he was an old man and *heavy*" (1 Samuel 4:18, emphasis added).

To be "heavy," or "weighty" in idiomatic parlance, was to be glorious, esteemed, and distinguished. It's an expression reminiscent of the Sixties accolade, "He's a heavy dude." The word described the opinion others had of a person—that person's reputation, honor, and glory.

The New Testament employs the same idiom, using an equivalent Greek word *doksa*, which means "heavy." The word has a wide range of meanings, but all correspond closely to the Hebrew word *kabod* and embody the same idea of "weight"—honor, distinction, and glory. (This is the idiom behind the title of C. S. Lewis's book, *The Weight of Glory*.)

Many years ago I was traveling in central Greece with a friend, John Landrith, and happened upon a small museum in the city of Berea. The curator was busily uncrating a new acquisition as we walked in the door. The crate contained a recently excavated tablet dating from the first century A.D., which honored a distinguished citizen of that day. The tablet was written in Greek and listed the man's contributions to his community—the civic duties and appointments in which he had distinguished himself and put his mark on the community. The litany ended with the phrase: "This was his weight (*doksa*)."

Samuel's "weight" was holiness, and the gravity of that godliness weighed on all who knew him. So much so that Samuel's hometown, Ramah, became known as "the place where a man of God dwells."

Would that our lives so reflect Jesus that we will make a similar mark on our neighborhoods and that the memory of our godliness will linger on. 🍃

More's the Pity

Nothing but infinite pity is sufficient for
the infinite pathos of life.
—AMY CARMICHAEL

WARM-UP: *1 Samuel 17:12–30*

*O*n orders from his father, David traveled to the Valley of Elah to take supplies to his brothers, who were "fighting against the Philistines." When he reached the camp, David found the Israelite army taking "its battle positions" on one side of the valley, while the Philistines were forming their own battle lines on the other side.

David ran to locate his brothers and was talking to them when they were interrupted by Goliath, "the Philistine champion from Gath," who yelled out a challenge from across the valley. Then, to the young shepherd's chagrin, he saw God's army turn and run.

"Who is this uncircumcised Philistine," David fumed, "that he should defy the armies of the living God?"

Eliab, David's oldest brother, reacted angrily to his presence and his response. "Why have you come down here? And with whom did you leave those few sheep in the desert? I know how conceited you are and how wicked your heart is; you came down only to watch the battle."

Commentators jump to David's defense, but who knows what David's motives were? David was an abused child.[13] Perhaps he *did* speak with arrogance. Perhaps his heart *was* proud and contemptuous of his brothers. Or perhaps he did come out of curiosity just to see the battle.

We have no idea what his thoughts and intentions were, which is exactly my point. No one could know David's motives and no one could judge his heart. Eliab was wrong to ascribe conceit to his brother and wrong to think he could see wickedness in David's heart. Such knowledge is beyond human ken.

Yet how easily I, like Eliab, overstep my limits and judge my brother's motives, forgetting that it is the Lord who searches the heart and examines the mind (Jeremiah 17:10). I cannot know what others intend, or what forces and dispositions surge within their hearts. I cannot know the passions that wage war within their souls or what passions they are resisting. Only God understands the heart, and His understanding is infinite.

Scripture is full of examples of people who made mistaken assumptions—like Job's friends, who were convinced his suffering was the result of sin. Only God sees the whole picture. With our limited human insight a faulty verdict is assured.

Instead of judging, we might better ask those who seem to go wrong, "Can you tell me why you did what you did?" We may be surprised at what we learn. And even if we can't fully understand another person's intentions, we may become more understanding. "The purposes of a man's heart are deep waters," reads the proverb, "but a man of understanding draws them out" (Proverbs 20:5). Or, as the old saying goes: "Know another's burden and you won't be able to speak except in pity."

Some years ago I heard a story about a young salesman who worked for a company whose president gave turkeys to all his employees at Christmas. On the day the turkeys were handed out, however, a couple of the man's friends stole the turkey tagged with his name and substituted a turkey made of papier-mâché. At the end of the day, the unsuspecting young salesman caught his bus for home, the bogus bird under his arm. The man was a bachelor and didn't cook, so the gift was a complication as far as he was concerned.

As it happened, he found himself seated next to a man whose melancholy was obvious. Feeling compassion for the stranger, the salesman began a conversation during which the other man's bitter circumstances began to unfold: he had lost his job and had almost no money for Christmas—only a few dollars with which to purchase groceries for Christmas dinner. His funds were insufficient for anything more than bare essentials.

The salesman sized up the situation and realized he could unload the turkey in a way that would be mutually beneficial. His first thought was to simply give the bird to the man. His second thought was to sell it to him for a few dollars, thinking that in this way his new acquaintance could salvage his dignity.

When the salesman explained that he had no use for the turkey and would be happy to let the man have it, the other man was elated. The exchange was made, and the man went off happily with Christmas dinner for his wife and children. And the well-meaning turkey vendor went home satisfied that he had done a good deed for the day.

When the young salesman returned to work after the holidays, however, he learned what his associates had done. Horrified, he could only imagine what that family must have thought when the package was unwrapped, the disappointment and anger when they discovered that the bird their desperate and despairing father had bought was a fraud. He devoted most of his free time for the next month trying to track down the victim of his unintended scam, but he never saw the man again.

The offended family must believe to this day that they were the victims of a cruel hoax—a classic example of man's inhumanity to man. But the fact is, the man's intentions were wholly good.

God will make the final judgment. Until then, we must show pity. We cannot judge what we cannot know.

So gently scan your brother man,
Still gentler sister woman;

59

Tho' they may gang a kennin wrang,[14]
To step aside is human:
One point must still be greatly dark—
The moving, *why they do it;*
And just as lamely can ye mark,
How far perhaps they rue it.

Who made the heart, 'tis He alone
Decidedly can try us;
He knows each chord, its various tone,
Each spring, its various bias:
Then at the balance let's be mute,
We never can adjust it;
What's done we partly may compute,
But know not what's resisted.

—Robert Burns

The Lord of the Dance

Mocked by one shallow wife . . .
All the same I dance my head off!
—John Berryman

WARM-UP: *1 Samuel 18:20–30;*
19:11–17; 2 Samuel 6:20–23

*M*ichal, according to Jewish tradition, was an extraordinarily beautiful young woman. Her husband, David, was a heroic young commander. Their story—Michal's infatuation with David, her father's bizarre double-dowry and his frenzied efforts to keep the lovers apart, Michal's courage in abetting David's escape from Saul's assassins, their fourteen-year separation while David was in exile—is the stuff of which great love stories are made. But there was no "happily ever after" for Michal and David.

The narrator hints at the seed of love's destruction, Michal's in-house idol (19:13), a seed that bore deadly fruit when David brought the ark of the covenant to Jerusalem. Let me explain.

According to the Chronicler, one of David's first acts as king was to retrieve the ark of the covenant from Kiriath Jearim, for, as David put it, "we did not seek it in the days of Saul" (1 Chronicles 13:3 NASB).[15] This comment alone sets David apart from Saul. David was a spiritual man; Saul was a secular man. Saul had no time for God, nor did he want God's reminding symbol nearby. For forty years, the ark of the covenant was ignored by Israel and her king.

Early in his rule, however, David retrieved the ark, and in doing so revealed his own passion for God. As the ark ascended to its resting place in Jerusalem, David, in ecstatic joy, began to dance and celebrate. He stripped off his vestments and, clad solely in his ephod (the short, belted tunic worn under his royal robes), began whirling like a dervish.[16] He divested himself of the symbols of nobility and majesty and worshiped as an ordinary man.

Michal looked out of her window and "saw King David leaping and dancing before the LORD; [and] she despised him in her heart" (2 Samuel 6:16 NASB). Note the emphasis of the narrator here: "King" David. In Michal's opinion, this was no way for a nobleman to act!

Thus, after David blessed his people and turned to bless his own household, he encountered his wife's bitter scorn and mockery: "How the king of Israel has distinguished himself today, disrobing in the sight of the slave girls of his servants as any vulgar fellow would!" Or, as my friend Bob Roe aptly paraphrases Michal's reaction: "There goes the man again, making an ass of himself. He ought to be wearing gorgeous robes which reach to the ground, sitting in a reviewing stand with a scepter in his hand, receiving an 'eyes right' as the procession marches by."

David's response to his wife was one of melancholy resignation, for he knew the inclination of her heart. "I must dance before the Lord," he replied. "God chose me—above your father and his house, by the way. He's the one who made me ruler over Israel and I will celebrate and worship before him. If that be humiliation, so be it."

Michal couldn't dance with David, and thus the two went their separate ways and their love for one another died. The narrator leaves us with a terse and poignant comment on the estrangement and unhappiness that would haunt Michal for the rest of her life: "And Michal the daughter of Saul had no children to the day of her death" (2 Samuel 6:23).

D. H. Lawrence, in his play *David*, presents Michal as a passionate, consuming woman who resented David's absorption with God, which I find an accurate insight. David's love for God drove a wedge between the two. Michal, like her father, had no love for David's God and thus she could not understand, nor could she share his love.

Eros lures men and women into marriage, but it cannot hold them if one partner loves God and the other does not. Though side-by-side in life, their inner paths inexorably diverge, for one is led toward God by His indwelling Spirit, while the flesh leads the other away. In the essential matter of life—God Himself—they have nothing in common, and in time both their hearts are broken. This is their inevitable tragedy.

"Do not be yoked together with unbelievers," wrote Paul (2 Corinthians 6:14). The metaphor is based on an Old Testament law that prohibited plowing with an "ox and a donkey yoked together" (Deuteronomy 22:10). This was a humane consideration, for the unequal gaits of the two animals would cause the yoke to chafe *both*.

God's design for marriage is born out of love, not bigotry or bias, for He would spare us such heartbreaking pain. This is wisdom from above. ❧

The Mills of God

Though the mills of God grind slowly,
Yet they grind exceeding small;
Though with patience He stands waiting,
With exactness grinds He all.

—FREDRICK VON LOGAU

WARM-UP: *1 Samuel 21:1–9;*
22:6–23; Psalm 52

*D*avid was on the run, trying to evade Saul's henchmen who were in hot pursuit. Under cover of darkness, David and a handful of his followers crept into the town of Nob, situated in the hills about five miles south of Gibeah where Saul had set up his court.

Nob was a small settlement, secluded and seldom visited, and though only an hour away from Gibeah was sheltered from Saul's insanity. There, eighty-five priests—simple, peaceful men—quietly went about their intercessory work. They were clergymen, not fighting men. The only weapon at hand was Goliath's sword, which David had deposited for safekeeping at Nob. It had been kept wrapped in a cloth and hidden in the place where Ahimelech, the high priest, hung his vestments, hidden because the Philistines had confiscated most of Israel's iron weapons.

David needed food for his men and a weapon for himself, so he appealed to Ahimelech for both. The high priest was aware of the dissension between Saul and David and was fearful of getting involved, but David allayed his suspicion by—well, by lying. He told Ahimelech that he was on a secret mission for Saul, pled the urgency of his cause, and assured Ahimelech that he and his men had not contracted any defilement that would bar them from eating the consecrated bread.

Ahimelech, thus assured, complied with David's request, giving him the priest's food and Goliath's sword . . . and David vamoosed. But as he left, he spotted Doeg the Edomite, Saul's chief mule-skinner, in the sanctuary where the bread was kept, and a cold chill passed through David's heart.[17] He knew his visit would be reported to the king. And it was.

> Saul, spear in hand, was seated under the tamarisk tree on the hill at Gibeah, with all his officials standing around him. Saul said to them, "Listen, men of Benjamin! Will the son of Jesse give all of you fields and vineyards? Will he make all of you commanders of thousands and commanders of hundreds? Is that why you have all conspired against me? No one tells me when my son makes a covenant with the son of Jesse. None of you is concerned about me or tells me that my son has incited my servant to lie in wait for me, as he does today."
>
> But Doeg the Edomite, who was standing with Saul's officials, said, "I saw the son of Jesse come to Ahimelech son of Ahitub at Nob. Ahimelech inquired of the LORD for him; he also gave him provisions and the sword of Goliath the Philistine" (1 Samuel 22:6–10).

Doeg informed on David and implicated the priests, neglecting to tell Saul that David had given the priests false information. He did so solely to ingratiate himself with Saul, and in this self-seeking act, he set into motion a terrible cycle of vengeance.

Saul, in one of his insane rages, ordered the priests to come to Gibeah, where he interrogated them and immediately condemned them to death. But not one of Saul's soldiers would raise his hand against the priests. So the king ordered Doeg the informer to carry out his bloody sentence. "You turn and strike down the priests," said Saul.

"So Doeg the Edomite turned and struck them down. That day he killed eighty-five men who wore the linen ephod. He also put to the sword Nob, the town of the priests, with its men and women, its children and infants, and its cattle, donkeys and sheep" (1 Samuel 22:18–19).

One priest escaped the massacre, however, and reported to David, who wept with grief and guilt. "That day, when Doeg the Edomite was there, I knew he would be sure to tell Saul," said David. "I am responsible for the death of your father's whole family" (1 Samuel 22:22).

Then savage thoughts stirred David's soul, visions of rough justice, retaliation, and revenge. But even as he brooded on Doeg's appalling act, David remembered a great truth, which he subsequently recorded in one of his psalms.[18]

Surely *God* will bring you down to everlasting ruin:
He will snatch you up and tear you from your tent;
He will uproot you from the land of the living (Psalm 52:5,
   emphasis added).

David's words tumbled out of his mind and onto the page. "*God* will bring you down, Doeg! *He* will snatch you up! *He* will tear you away! *He* will root you up! *His* is the avenging day. *His* is the fierce and final wrath! Think about that!"

"Don't get mad, get even!" is the counsel of the culture these days, but like most conventional wisdom it is folly. Vendettas, once started, take on a life of their own, creating greater and greater wrong.

The infamous Hatfield-McCoy feud, which began with a dispute over the ownership of two razor-backed hogs, became a bloody vendetta that ran on unabated for several decades, decimating both West Virginia-Kentucky clans and bringing heartache to every family in the valley of the Tug Fork River. The men who started this bitter, destructive violence, Anse Hatfield and Ran'l McCoy, though responsible for scores of deaths, were never brought to justice and lived long, prosperous lives, an irony that's almost always overlooked in the telling and retelling of this tale.

Our vengeance—no matter how just our cause—quickly and surely runs amok. Only God has the wisdom and forbearance to redress evil and bring evil-doers to justice. He treads the winepress of His wrath *alone!* (Isaiah 63:3).

"Do not repay anyone evil for evil," warns the apostle Paul. "Do not take revenge, my friends, but leave room for God's wrath, for it is written: 'It is mine to avenge; *I will repay,*' says the Lord" (Romans 12:17, 19, italics added).

Retribution is inherent in the universe. The Lord of Hosts will have a day of reckoning (cf. Isaiah 2:12). ❦

The Man of Shame

With grief my just reproach I bear,
Shame fills me at the thought.
—WILLIAM COWPER

WARM-UP: *2 Samuel 4:4; 9:1–13*

*J*onathan, the son of King Saul, had a son whose name was Meribaal. He was five years old when news of Jonathan's death came from Gilboa. His nurse, expecting the Philistines to overrun the citadel, snatched up the child and fled, but in her panic she fell and the child was severely injured. As a result, he "became crippled," the beginning of a tortured, melancholy life. His humiliation was so deep that his name was changed from Meribaal ("The Lord is my Advocate") to Mephibosheth (*mephi* means something like "my brokenness" and *bosheth* means "shame").

"We shouldn't take names to ourselves," Tolkien's Frodo said to the self-pitying creature, Sméagol. "It's unwise whether true or false." But Mephibosheth couldn't avoid the name change. He thought of himself as a ruined man, and in all his utterances he speaks as a weary, dispirited soul.

Some years later, David recalled an oath he had sworn to Jonathan: "Show me unfailing kindness like that of the LORD as long as I live ... and do not ever cut off your kindness from my family. ... And Jonathan had David reaffirm his oath out of love for him" (1 Samuel 20:14–15, 17).

David determined to keep his word to his dear friend, so he asked Saul's old servant, Ziba, if any of Jonathan's descendants still lived. "Oh, yes," Ziba replied. "One of Jonathan's sons is still alive, but he's crippled in both feet."

David immediately had Mephibosheth brought to him from exile (Mephibosheth was living across the Jordan, far from the family estate and David's court) and welcomed him into his presence.

"Mephibosheth!" the king cried with joy when he saw the son of his old friend.

"Your servant," Mephibosheth replied as he fell to his knees, thinking that David would surely kill him. (It was the custom in other cultures then to kill all presumptive heirs to the throne.)

But David said, "Don't be afraid, Mephibosheth. You will eat at my table for the rest of your life."

We see our story in Mephibosheth's. As David himself put it, this is "the love of the LORD."[19] God does not say, "Learn to walk well and I'll take you in." He loves us as David loved Mephibosheth—*as is*. We stagger and falter, we stumble and fall, yet He receives us and invites us to eat at His table.

Our decision to come to Him may be nothing more than the desperate culmination of a lifetime of failure. We may have struggled so long with our fallen and failed nature that we've given up. But God does not despair of us even when we've despaired of ourselves. "He is eternal," Augustine said, "therefore His love endures forever."

Some of us are so broken that our personalities resist change. Yet God discerns the possibilities in the most damaged life. He can take all that's unworthy in it and, as it pleases Him, gradually turn it into good, though for reasons known only to God, some of us may glorify Him for a time through our brokenness. Some of us are so handicapped that complete healing awaits heaven's cure. Yet we can be assured today of God's everlasting favor and love.

Mephibosheth "*always* ate at the king's table, [though] he was crippled in both feet," the narrator concludes (2 Samuel 9:13, italics added). Mephibosheth never walked as a man should walk, but he always had a place at the king's table.

And the tablecloth covered his feet.[20] ❦

The Legacy of Lust

I polluted my life with the sewage of lust.
—AUGUSTINE

WARM-UP: *2 Samuel 13*

*P*ride makes us believe we can find the answers, said Pascal, and lust makes us look for answers in the wrong places. Amnon's story documents Pascal's dictum.

Amnon was David's first-born child, the son of Ahinoam, one of David's wives. Tamar was the daughter of Maacah, another of David's wives, and thus Amnon's half-sister.

I won't supply the details; you can read those for yourself in the Scripture passage. It's enough to say that Amnon's lust led him to rape his sister. Then, we're told, Amnon's lust turned to hatred. "Get this woman out of here," he shouted to his servants. "And bolt the door after her."

Our English versions don't, and perhaps can't, capture the deep contempt expressed in the Hebrew text. The phrase "this woman" is really just the word for "this!"—referring not to a person but to a thing. (In recent years, we've heard a version of this from one of our own presidents: "I never had sexual relations with *that* woman!") The dehumanizing demonstrative is then followed in the Hebrew text with a contemptuous expression, used to dismiss those whose presence is unusually offensive and obnoxious.

Lust quickly turns into revulsion. One rabbinical commentary notes that Amnon simply "projected onto Tamar the hatred which now he felt for himself."

Shakespeare makes the same point in one of his sonnets:

Th' expense of spirit in a waste of shame
Is lust in action, and till action, lust
Is perjur'd, murd'rous, bloody, full of blame,
Savage, extreme, rude, cruel, not to trust,
Enjoy'd no sooner but despised straight,
Past reason hunted, and no sooner had,
Past reason hated as a swallowed bait
On purpose laid to make the taker mad . . . .
—Sonnet 129, 1–8

Shakespeare breaks lust down into its "before" and "after" components and concludes that lust leads to actions that deplete us of "spirit," which leads to shame and self-loathing. We then redirect that self-blame at others. We despise ourselves and detest the objects of our lust.

At Amnon's directive, his servant threw Tamar out of the room and locked her out, even though "she was wearing a richly ornamented robe, for this was the kind of garment the virgin daughters of the king wore." Though Tamar was a princess, Amnon treated her like a tramp. And Tamar went out weeping aloud, shamed and broken, her life ruined.

The legacy of Amnon's lust was tragic and far-reaching: Tamar's brother Absalom bided his time and two years later killed their brother Amnon, an act of treachery for which David banished him, but that's another story.

The lesson is clear: unbridled passion brings ruin to others and to ourselves. Unlike David, we cannot excuse it or pass over it. We must deal with it.

The place to begin is with our minds, for that's where sin begins: "The good man brings good things out of the good stored up in him, and the evil man brings evil things out of the evil stored up in him" (Matthew 12:35). Or, as an old proverb states, "As a man thinks in his heart so is he" (Proverbs 23:7).

Sexually stimulating images abound in our world. It's impossible to evade them. And even when we do for a short time, memory conjures them up. As an old woman in one of Aesop's fables reminisced, "Ah, what memories cling 'round the instruments of our pleasure."

Simon Stylites, an early Christian monk, spent several years of his life perched atop a fifty-foot pole hoping to avoid the temptations of the flesh. It was a well-meant but meaningless exercise. He was tormented at night by mental images of dancing girls. *C'est la vie!*

Libido is part of our God-given make-up, and finds its biblical and rightful place in marriage. But there are moments when our minds are directed to someone other than our mate and sexual thoughts are awakened. That first reaction is mere *temptation* to sin, not sin itself. The thought only becomes sin when we bring it into sharper focus, fix on it, reflect on it, and fantasize about it.

Jesus pointed out that we have sinned when we have looked at a woman *in order* "to lust after her" (Matthew 5:28 KJV).[21] The first look is not sin; it becomes sin when we linger and let the look pass into imagination. Lustful thoughts come unbidden, but we must not entertain them. "We cannot stop birds from flying over our heads," Martin Luther said, "but we can keep them from building nests in our hair."

When lustful thoughts come, we must turn immediately to God and yield those thoughts to Him. Deflect the initial stimuli into prayer, thanksgiving, and praise for beauty, turning thought into prayer for the person who captures our attention. Prayer converts primal lust into a purer love.

Above all, the pursuit of God serves best to quiet our more insistent sexual drives. Worship and adoration of Christ sublimate our other passions.

There is a connection between human sexuality and human spirituality. Charles Williams observed: "Sensuality and sanctity are so closely intertwined that our motives in some cases can hardly be separated until the tares are gathered out of the wheat by heavenly wit." Sexual passion, as George MacDonald said, is "a passion on the breast / and something deeper that cannot be expressed."

The mysterious, inexplicable power of sexual passion is essentially a hunger for God—a hunger that originates in God. It is His calling, His wooing that awakens us to desire. Our sexual hungers are essentially the answering cry of our hearts to His call. As G. K. Chesterton said, "Even when men knock on the door of a brothel they are looking for God."

God, thus, is the source of our passions, but He is also their satisfaction. Intimacy with Him serves to assuage the raw passions of the flesh. "Assuage," I say, not "fully satisfy," for final satisfaction awaits heaven and home. But the healing process can begin here and now.

Take me to You, imprison me, for I—
Except You enthrall me—never shall be free,
Never ever chaste, except you ravish me.
                                    —John Donne's prayer

The Queen of Sheba

Sheba was never more covetous of wisdom
and fair virtue
Than this poor soul shall be.
—WILLIAM SHAKESPEARE

WARM-UP: *1 Kings 10:1–13*

*A*ccording to tradition, her name was Makeda, which means "Greatness," and she was the reigning monarch of Sheba, a vast Arabian kingdom roughly corresponding to present-day Yemen and Ethiopia. Sheba was a great trading nation, located at the southern terminus of the "Spice Road" that originated in the Far East and dominated Red Sea and Indian Ocean trade.

Perhaps the queen's merchants encountered Israel's God in their journeys. Or Solomon's mariners who sailed from Aqaba may have mentioned the name of the Lord. Whatever the source of the witness, in some way Makeda heard, was intrigued, and traveled to Israel to ply Solomon with "hard questions."

According to the *Kebra Negast*, the national-religious history of Ethiopia, Sheba was a center of sun and moon worship and the queen was the nation's high priestess. (Recent excavations at Ma'rib, Sheba's capital, have revealed an imposing temple to the moon god.) But something was missing from Makeda's heart— something that strength, dominion, hoarded wealth, and all the Sabean gods could not satisfy. So she came to Solomon looking for that elusive "something more."

Josephus said she was "inquisitive into philosophy," but her questions seem more personal than philosophical, for, as the text puts it, she had heard about Solomon "and his relation[ship] to the . . . LORD." Hers were not questions of the mind, but of the "heart" (1 Kings 10:2 NASB).

Sheba learned from Solomon that the Lord is a "compassionate and gracious God, slow to anger, abounding in love and faithfulness, maintaining love to thousands, and forgiving wickedness, rebellion and sin" (Exodus 34:6-7). She saw "the burnt offerings [Solomon] made at the temple of the LORD" (1 Kings 10:5) and realized that she could be made pure. "She heard fair truth distilling, Its expression choice and thrilling, From a tongue so soft and killing,"[22] and she was speechless (10:5). There was nothing more to ask or say. Solomon had given her "all she desired" (10:13).

The text tells us no more, though ancient traditions report that the queen gave her heart to the Lord. But we have a more sure word, for Jesus set His seal on her faith when He charged His detractors with these words: "The Queen of the South will rise at the judgment with this generation and condemn it; for she came from ends of the earth to listen to Solomon's wisdom, and now one greater than Solomon is here" (Matthew 12:42). Makeda journeyed 1400 miles to hear from God, while the scribes and Pharisees would not cross the street to listen to Him.

Furthermore, Sheba's pilgrimage became the paradigm from which is drawn the picture of all nations gathering to Israel's Messiah in the last days. "The kings of Sheba . . . will present him gifts," wrote Solomon. "All kings will bow down to him and all nations will serve him. For he will deliver the needy who cry out, the afflicted who have no one to help"(Psalm 72:10–12; see also Isaiah 2:2–4).

All of which reminds me that there are luminaries in my sphere of influence who may seem to have no interest in God but who secretly long for wisdom and virtue. These are the poor souls whose tears run down inside, the afflicted who have no one to help, who live in hunger and melancholy weariness for which they know no cure.

You never know. ❦

What Is Written Is Written

The truly wise man is the one who believes the Bible against the opinions of any man. If the Bible says one thing, and any body of men says another, he will decide, "This book is the word of him that cannot lie."

—R. A. TORREY

WARM-UP: *1 Kings 13*

*J*osephus, the Jewish historian, said his name was Jadon, but no one knows for sure. We only know him as "a man of God" who "by the word of God . . . came from Judah to Bethel" (1 Kings 13:1).

God sent Jadon to pronounce judgment against Jeroboam, the king of Israel who had put God behind him. The young prophet appeared at Jeroboam's altar at Bethel and promised that good king Josiah would profane Jeroboam's worship center (a prediction fulfilled about three hundred years later), and sealed that promise with a sign. Jeroboam's ersatz altar disintegrated right in front of his eyes!

Jadon was clearly a prophet—a man who carried God's word.

Jeroboam tried to restrain the prophet, first by threat and then by bribe, but the young man of God was uncompromising: "Even if you were to give me half your possessions," he said, "I would not go with you, nor would I eat bread or drink water here. For I was commanded by the word of the LORD: 'You must not eat bread or drink water or return by the way you came.'" So he took another road and did not return by the way he had come to Bethel" (13:7–10). Let's hear it for Jadon! No concession. No capitulation. He walked into Jeroboam's court and out again, unscathed, true to the truth.

But on the way home, Jadon encountered another so-called prophet—a decaying old derelict, supported by Jeroboam's court and paid to keep his mouth shut—who had come out to entice him.

"Are you the man of God who came from Judah?" he asked.

"I am," [Jadon] replied.

"So the prophet said to him, 'Come home with me and eat.'

"The man of God said, 'I cannot turn back and go with you, nor can I eat bread or drink water with you in this place. I have been told by the word of the LORD: "You must not eat bread or drink water there or return by the way you came."'

"The old prophet answered, 'I too am a prophet, as you are. And an angel said to me by the word of the LORD: "Bring him back with you to your house so that he may eat bread and drink water."'" (But he was lying to him.) So the man of God returned with him and ate and drank in his house" (13:14-19).

Later, at dinner, the word of the Lord did come to the old prophet, and he cried out to the man of God who had come from Judah: "This is what the LORD says, 'You have defied the word of the LORD and have not kept the commandment the LORD your God gave you'" (13:21).

The young man's doom was foretold. Truth is truth, whether spoken by Jesus or by a reprobate.

That evening, as Jadon made his way home, a lion stalked and killed him. When travelers found his carcass, with the lion still standing over the kill, they reported the unnatural incident in the city. And when the old prophet heard the story he spoke the truth once more: "It is the man of God who defied the word of the LORD. The LORD has given him over to the lion, which has mauled him and killed him, as the word of the LORD had warned him" (13:26).

And so the old scoundrel buried the prophet from Bethel in his own tomb, with the proviso that others someday bury his bones with those of the man of God. For, he said, "The message he declared by the word of the LORD against the altar in Bethel and against all the shrines on the high places in the towns of Samaria will certainly come true" (13:32).

And it did: Josiah demolished Jeroboam's altar and high place and desecrated the tombs of his false prophets, "in accordance with the word of the LORD proclaimed by *the man of God who foretold these things*" (2 Kings 23:16, emphasis added). Josiah spared the bones of the prophet from Judah and those of the old man with him.

You can't help but wonder why God was so severe with this young man. He was devoted. He was a man of God who delivered the word of God. And then having done his job, wearied by the journey, hungry, thirsty, relaxing for a moment under a tree, he was overwhelmed by sudden seduction and swept away. Was his deviation so bad? Surely God understood his frame.

And indeed He did. He took him home to be with Him forever. But on this occasion the stakes were too high for God to go soft on Jadon's disobedience. Jeroboam must know that God says what He means and means it! Judgment was pronounced and judgment could not be averted. The fate of the nation was at stake. If God had winked at the prophet's wrongdoing, Jeroboam might not have known the enormity of his transgression and the severity with which it would be judged. No, God could not overlook His prophet's sin.

Jeroboam did not listen and thus grew into a prime Old Testament example of an evil, idolatrous king. But *we* must listen and we must hear. What is written is written. Once written, God does not modify His word. The old man came claiming a new revelation: An *angel* had up-dated God's word! It sounded likely; it looked real; perhaps the old prophet had seen an angel. Satan does masquerade as an angel of light (2 Corinthians 11:14). But as Paul so urgently wrote: "Even if we or an angel from heaven should preach a gospel other than the one we [the apostles] preached to you, let him be eternally condemned" (Galatians 1:8–9).

So, we do not "run ahead," John said, we go back (2 John 9). John was inveighing against certain deceivers for whom everything was flexible and up for grabs. They were progressive in their thinking, always looking for a newer, better word. But, as John insists, we go back to the inspired word, "that which was from the beginning," back to the prophets, back to Jesus and what His apostles saw and heard, back to the truth "once for all delivered" to the saints (Jude 3 NASB).

John implores us: "Test the spirits to see whether they are from God" (1 John 4:1). 🍂

Legacy

As for Omri, king of Israel,
he humbled Moab many years.
—THE STELE OF KING MESHA
OF MOAB (830 B.C.)

WARM-UP: *1 Kings 16:21–28*

*C*arolyn asked me what I was doing today. "Writing an essay on the life of Omri," I said.

"Who?" she replied.

Exactly!

From a political standpoint, Omri was the most notable of Israel's kings. Ancient Near East monuments remark on his military and political genius, and for two hundred years after his death, Israel was known as "Omri-land."

Yet Omri is given only eight verses in the Bible, and the historic assessment of his achievements is that he was a loser, an historical verdict reminiscent of Percy Bysshe Shelley's poem about King Ozymandias, whose shattered monument had crumbled round "two vast and trunkless legs of stone." Upon the pedestal these words appeared: "My name is Ozymandias, King of Kings: Look on my works, ye mighty, and despair!" Shelley reflects:

> Nothing beside remains. Round the decay
> Of that colossal wreck, boundless and bare
> The lone and level sands stretch far away.

Oh, yes, Omri did build Israel's magnificent capital city, Samaria, with its imposing acropolis, citadel, colonnaded approaches, and terraced gardens, and for that he is vaguely remembered. But "nothing… remains." Ancient Samaria has crumbled into dust.

All of which reminds me that few things remain in this life, apropos of which a friend of mine gave me a test the other day. He asked me to name:

- the five wealthiest men in the world
- the last four Heisman trophy winners
- the last three winners of the Miss America contest
- the names of two people who have won a Nobel or Pulitzer prize
- any one of last year's Oscar winners

Then he asked me to name:

- the person who brought me to faith
- two people who have wept and walked with me through dark days
- three teachers who have stirred me to love God's Word
- four friends who have touched me with unconditional love
- five men and women whose godliness has caused me to hunger for God

These are the righteous who "will be remembered forever" (Psalm 112:6). Theirs is the fruit that *remains.* 🌿

Saying Our Prayers

"What should I do then, mem?"
"Go your way, laddie . . . and say your prayers."
—GEORGE MACDONALD

WARM-UP: *2 Kings 4:1–7*

*J*osephus, the Jewish historian, suggested that this woman was the wife of Obadiah, that good man who provided food and shelter for the persecuted prophets during Ahab's reign. It could be, but the Hebrew text simply describes her as "the wife of a man from the company of the prophets"—one anonymous, unremarkable woman who became the victim of circumstances beyond her control.

This woman's story is one of accumulated grief. First, her husband died, leaving her destitute and deeply in debt. Then her creditors came knocking on the door, demanding that she pay up or sell her two sons into slavery to compensate them. Immediately, and with sound wisdom, she went to Elisha, the embodiment of God's presence in the land.

When Elisha heard this woman's plea for help, he did not rush to meet her need. Had he done so, she might have gained a little comfort, but not from the highest source; and she would have gained it too soon for her highest good. No, Elisha instead said to the woman, "Go outside, borrow vessels of all your neighbors, empty vessels and not too few. Then go in, and shut the door upon yourself and your sons, and pour into all these vessels; and when one is full, set it aside" (2 Kings 4:3–4, paraphrase).

When I read the prophet's words, I think of Jesus' words, "When you pray, go into your room, *close the door* and pray to your

Father, who is unseen. Then your Father, who sees what is done in secret, will reward you" (Matthew 6:6). This is the hidden life of prayer.

Oh, I know, nothing is said about prayer in the Old Testament account, but it's interesting to me that Jesus' verb, translated "close the door," roughly corresponds to the Greek version of 2 Kings, the version Jesus Himself read and frequently quoted. Could it be that He had this story in mind? If so, I suggest that prayer, in our Lord's mind, involves shutting yourself up with God and relying solely on *His* resources in your time of need. In other words, prayer is the highest expression of our utter dependence on God.

So, to get back to the story, the woman and her sons gathered jars from the neighborhood and went about their business, "doing what lay before them while praying; and praying while doing it," F. B. Meyer said. They poured until all the jars were filled. Then the widow sold the oil, paid her debts, and lived on the remainder.

May I press the analogy to make a point? It strikes me that the best thing I can do for another person is to teach him or her to pray. My task is not to find answers or fix people, but to get them in touch with God, for the only real help I can give is to bring others to the One who is able to help (Hebrews 4:16).

That's why I pray with those who bring their burdens to me. That's why I pray with those who grieve for their wayward children. That's why I pray with others when they have no answers to life's hard questions. I pray *for* them, but I'm teaching them *to* pray—to take their needs to the only One who can help them.

We must love much and listen well and use every occasion of need to teach others to pray. This is our calling: to bring men and women, boys and girls into the presence of God. This is heaven's cure for earth's deepest needs. ❧

The Man from Baal Shalisha

What matter though our loaves be few?
Alike the little and the much
When He shall add to what we have
His multiplying touch.

—ANNIE JOHNSON FLINT

WARM-UP: *2 Kings 4:42–44*

*B*aal Shalisha was a region in the tribal allotment of Benjamin. In earlier times the region was known simply as "Shalisha" (1 Samuel 9:4), but with the advent of Jezebel's Baalism the name of the region was changed to *Baal* Shalisha to express devotion to her pagan god.

Shalisha is the number "three" in Hebrew, used in Semitic imagery to express plurality. It signifies "a rounding out," or "completion." In other words, in pagan thought, Baal was the god that had it all together.

A certain man from Baal Shalisha, however, had another idea. He had labored over his fields—plowed the soil, planted the crops, fertilized and irrigated and reaped the results. Yet this man knew it was Yahweh, not Baal, who gave the grain, new wine, and oil. To show his gratitude he brought the first fruits of his harvest to God's prophet Elisha: a few loaves of barley bread baked from the first ripe grain, along with some heads of new grain.

The "firstfruits" was the ten percent given to support the clergy in Israel (Numbers 18:13; Deuteronomy 18:4). The prophets and priests had no "inheritance" in Israel (no land to claim, no fields to work), for their calling was to devote themselves to caring for others. So this man from Baal Shalisha brought his offering to the prophet, and it was enough to sustain him for a season.

This offering was an unexpected provision in a time of profound need. Elisha, like others in Israel, was hard-pressed by the drought. But the prophet determined that he would share this gift with others. His servant pointed out his improvidence: the gift would supply Elisha's immediate needs, but if he set it before "a hundred men" he would lose any good from the loaves. There simply was not enough to go around.

Nevertheless, Elisha commanded his servant, "Give it to the people to eat," adding a promise that this scanty provision would amply supply. "This is what the LORD says: 'They will eat and have some left over.'"

The verb translated "have some left over" means "to have more than enough,"[23] and the grammar suggests an axiom: *When God gives, He gives more than enough.*

True to God's word, when Elisha's servant set the loaves before the people, "they ate and had some left over" (2 Kings 4:44). There was enough—and more than enough.[24]

At times there are good reasons to say no to a need or to a request, but we should never say no merely because we feel inadequate.

"We have few loaves," we say.

"Give them to Me," our Lord replies. "They are more than enough." ❦

Things Both Great and Small

"It's very hard to be brave,
when you're Very Small."
—PIGLET IN *WINNIE THE POOH*

WARM-UP: *2 Kings 5:1–14*

*S*tormin' Naaman was the commander of the Syrian army. He was a mighty warrior, highly regarded by the king of Syria and held in high esteem by his nation.

Rabbinic tradition holds that Naaman was the anonymous soldier at the battle of Ramoth Gilead whose random arrow mortally wounded Ahab, the king of Israel (1 Kings 22:34), and for that reason Syria's victory was attributed to him (2 Kings 5:1). This may have been the "lucky" shot that brought him to the king's attention and enabled him to rise through the ranks to become commander of the army.

Naaman had honor, celebrity, and power, but he was a leper. We don't know what stage his leprosy had reached, but eventually his body would become discolored and deformed, corrupted by lesions and stumps, shocking in its ugliness, a gross, grisly caricature of what a man was intended to be. Leprosy is one of earth's most appalling diseases. It's treatable today, but in Naaman's time it was terminal—a living death of isolation and loneliness.

But God had a solution for Naaman, and it began with the love of a little girl. We don't know her name; she was only a slave, taken captive from the land of Israel.

The story in Scripture is concise: nothing is said about the terror of the girl's abduction, the sorrow of separation from her family, her homesickness, or the crushing grief of her parents. Nor is there any hint of that bitter rage against her enemy that sometimes goes by the name of holy zeal. She saw her servitude as an opportunity to serve God, an opportunity that came with the terminal illness of her master.

Instead of thinking of his disease as poetic justice, as some in her situation might do, she sought to help Naaman, to bring him to God, which is the only help that any of us can give.

The little girl said to her mistress, "If only my master would see the prophet who is in Samaria! He would cure him of his leprosy" (5:3). Jewish rabbis call attention to the peculiar construction of this sentence and translate it, "If only the *supplications* of my master could be set before the prophet who is in Samaria," which suggests Naaman's quiet desperation. He was a hard man, but underneath his tough exterior was terrible despair. He was praying to his gods, even as he was dying, and there was nothing anyone on earth could do.

Naaman's wife reported the little slave girl's comment to her husband—and amazingly, he believed her. Immediately he sought permission from the king to visit Samaria. The king sent him off with a military escort and a letter to the king of Israel, which said in part, "With this letter I am sending my servant Naaman to you so that you may cure him of his leprosy" (5:6).

The intent of the letter was to put Naaman in touch with the prophet Elisha, since in those days oriental kings were in close contact with their prophets and priests. The king of Syria assumed that this was the case in Israel and that Joram would simply hand the case over to his prophet.

But Joram didn't believe in God's prophet and assumed that everything depended on him. He read the letter, tore his robes in fear, and wailed, "Am I God? Can I kill and bring back to life? Why does this fellow send someone to *me* to be cured of his leprosy? See how he is trying to pick a quarrel with me!" (5:7, emphasis added).

Ben-Hadad, king of Syria, took the little girl's word's seriously. Joram didn't. The king of Israel knew more about the living God but believed less than his pagan counterpart.

Somehow, Elisha got wind of the matter and sent word to Joram "Have the man come to me and he will know that there is a prophet in Israel" (5:8). So Naaman and his entourage, his horses and chariots, rode to the door of Elisha's house. But the prophet didn't even come out to meet him. Instead, he sent out a messenger to announce God's word to Naaman: "Go, wash yourself seven times in the Jordan, and your flesh will be restored and you will be cleansed" (5:10).

Elisha was not intimidated by Naaman, nor was he untouched by his infirmity. By making himself invisible, he was demonstrating that he had nothing to do with the cure. It was the work of God.

Naaman, however, had another perspective: "I thought that he [Elisha] would surely come out to me and stand and call on the name of the LORD his God, wave his hand over the spot and cure me of my leprosy. Are not Abana and Pharpar, the rivers of Damascus, better than any of the waters of Israel? Couldn't I wash in them and be cleansed?" he grumbled (5:11–12).

Naaman thought the prophet would come out of his house and put on a spectacular show—prance and dance, do a little hocus-pocus, mutter a few magic words. After all, Naaman was a very important man. (The verb translated "surely come" indicates that he thought that Elisha, whom he regarded as his social inferior, had an obligation to come out to meet him. Furthermore, the phrase "to me" is in an emphatic position in the sentence, suggesting "to someone like me.")

Elisha not only failed to put in an appearance, he also further embarrassed Naaman, at least from the Syrian's perspective, by insisting that he bathe in Israel's miserable river. Naaman had crossed the Jordan, a gray-green, sluggish body of water that looked like liquid mud. Indeed, the rivers of Damascus that ran from the snowfields of Lebanon were much more inviting. In outraged pride he stalked away from the word of God—unchanged.

Fortunately, some of Naaman's servants intervened, "If the prophet had told you to do some great thing, would you not have done it?" they implored. "How much more, then, when he tells you, 'Wash and be cleansed'! So he went down and dipped himself in the Jordan seven times, as the man of God had told him, and his flesh was restored and became clean like that of a young boy" (5:13–14). The Hebrew text concludes with the phrase: "and he was clean."

Naaman's ultimate response was faith and worship. "Now I know," he said, "that there is no God in all the world except in Israel." And behind his faith, unseen and unknown, stood the love of a little girl.

So what if you're Very Small. Be strong. You can do great things if you do them with God's love. ❦

The Would-Be Woodcutter

When I would beget contentment . . . I walk the meadows
and there contemplate the little creatures that are cared for
by the goodness of God.

—Izaak Walton

WARM-UP: *2 Kings 6:1–7*

The school of the prophets at Gilgal had swelled to over a
hundred men (2 Kings 4:43); and their settlements at Bethel
and Jericho had grown to such numbers that their meeting place
had become too small. Someone suggested to Elisha that the men
should go to the woods, cut logs, and enlarge their facilities. The
prophet agreed and was invited to accompany them.

The woodcutters made their way up the Jordan Valley to the
spot where they planned to fell trees and float them downriver to
the building site. Things were going well until, as Matthew Henry
so quaintly put it, "one of them, accidentally fetching too fierce a
stroke (as those who work seldom are apt to be too violent), threw
off his ax-head into the water."

"Oh, my lord," the man cried, "it was borrowed!"

"Where did it go?" Elisha asked.

When the man showed him the place, Elisha cut a stick,
reached with it into the water, and "made the iron float [flow]."

"Lift it out," he said.

The man "reached out his hand and took it."

Some have suggested that nothing miraculous happened.
Elisha simply probed in the water with his stick until he located
the ax-head and dragged it into sight. But if that were the case,
such a common incident would hardly have been worth reporting.

No, it was a miracle: Elisha caused the ax-head to "flow" as the Hebrew text says. The ax-head was set in motion by a sudden rush of the water so that it drifted out of deep water and into the shallows where he could retrieve it.

This miracle enshrines a simple and profound truth: God cares about the small stuff of life—lost ax-heads, lost coins, lost keys, lost files, lost contact lenses—all the little things that cause us to fret and worry. He doesn't always restore what was misplaced (He has reasons of His own), but He understands our loss and comforts us in our distress.

I think of those times when our grandchildren grieve over some small loss and my own heart is touched with their grief. The broken or mislaid item is usually some trifling thing, some toy or trinket—but it isn't trifling to them. The item has no meaning for me, but the loss matters to me because it matters to them . . . and my grandchildren matter to me.

And so it is with our Father. Our small worries mean everything to Him because *we* mean everything to Him. We can cast all our care on Him because He cares about *us* (1 Peter 5:7).

Does Jesus care when my heart is pained
Too deeply for mirth and song,
As the burdens press, and the cares distress,
And the way grows weary and long?

O yes, He cares, I know He cares!
His heart is touched with my grief;
When the days are weary, the long nights dreary,
I know my Savior cares.

—Frank E. Graeff

Try, Try, Try Again

If at first you don't succeed, try, try again!
—W. E. HICKSON

WARM-UP: *2 Kings 13:10–19*

*K*ing Jehoash went down to Elisha's house to seek his dying counsel. "My father!" he cried, as he bent over the old prophet. "[Where are] the chariots and horsemen of Israel!" (2 Kings 13:14).

The army of Israel had been reduced to fifty horsemen and ten chariots and ten thousand foot soldiers (2 Kings 13:7). They were powerless against the Syrian army, which was now backed by the super-power, Assyria. With Elisha's death, Jehoash believed that even the few horsemen and chariots of God would depart and he would be left alone to face impossible odds.

Elisha responded with a symbolic action, instructing the king to "Get a bow and some arrows." When the king had taken up the weapon, Elisha "put his hands on the kings hands" and commanded him: "Take the bow in your hands, open the east window [in the direction of the enemy] and shoot!" (13:16–17).

Shooting an arrow in the direction of an enemy was an ancient way of declaring war. This was also Elisha's way of encouraging Jehoash to take action, to vigorously prosecute the war against Syria. And by placing his hands on the young king's hands, the prophet assured Jehoash that the strength of the shot came from the Lord, just as an adult might put his hands on a child's hands and pull a bow too powerful for him to draw.

Then Elisha sealed the symbol with the prediction that the king and his army would defeat Syria in battle. "The LORD'S arrow of victory, the arrow of victory over Aram!" Elisha declared. "You will completely destroy the Arameans [Syrians] at Aphek" (2 Kings 13:17).

But there was more. Elisha said to the king, "Take the remaining arrows from your quiver and shoot an arrow into the ground." Jehoash did this three times and then stopped.

Elisha was indignant. "You should have struck the ground five or six times [you should have shot all the arrows in your quiver]," he fumed. "Then you would have defeated Aram and completely destroyed it. But now you will defeat it only three times" (2 Kings 13:19).

And so it was: "Jehoash son of Jehoahaz recaptured from Ben-Hadad son of Hazael the towns he had taken in battle from his father Jehoahaz. *Three times* Jehoash defeated him" (13:25, italics added).

Though Jehoash won three battles, he lost the war. Aram continued to intimidate and menace Israel until Israel finally made peace with them, entering into a treaty that eventually led to the treacherous assault on their own brothers in Judah (cf. 2 Kings 15:37ff. and Isaiah 7:1–2).

There's a principle imbedded in the story: "If at first you don't succeed, try, try again."

Most of you will never be called to do battle with Syrian soldiers, but I'm certain that you're presently engaged in battle with personal enemies—"sinful desires, which war against your soul" (1 Peter 2:11). Perhaps you have an uncontrolled temper, an alcohol or drug addiction, a sexual perversion, a tendency toward sloth, greed, malice, bitterness, or sullen, stubborn pride.

The first step is to declare war against the enemy. Never give in to a sinful habit that has taken up residence in your life. Declare all-out war! There can be no neutrality and certainly no surrender. Determine that you will *never* make peace with the flesh. To do so is to invite disaster. You will master sin or be mastered by it. There is no middle ground.

The second step is to remind yourself that God is a hands-on God. It is by His power and might that you will be set free. Without *Him* you do *nothing*.

And finally, never give up. Keep drawing the bow; keep striking a blow! It is through faith and patience that you will receive the promises. If nothing else, your struggle against sin will cause you to turn to God again and again and cling to Him in desperation, which may, in the end, be worth far more to God than present deliverance, for what He wants most of all is your dependence and love.

It may be that your struggle will continue until death, or until the Lord comes. Certainly there will be times when you will get discouraged. But you must never give up.

John White writes in *The Fight:* "There is no place for giving up. The warfare is so much bigger than our personal humiliations. To feel sorry for oneself is totally inappropriate. Over such a soldier I would pour a bucket of icy water. I would drag him to his feet, kick him in the rear end, put a sword in his hand, and shout, 'Now fight!' In some circumstances one must be cruel to be kind. What if you have fallen for a tempting ruse of the Enemy? What if you're not the most brilliant swordsman in the army? You hold Excaliber in your hand! Get behind the lines for a break if you're too weak to go on, strengthen yourself with a powerful draught of the wine of Romans 8:1–4. Then get back into the fight before your muscles get stiff!"[25]

What's required of us is dogged endurance through the ebbs and flows, ups and downs, victories and losses of life, knowing that God is working in us to accomplish His purpose. We must staunchly, steadfastly, persistently pursue God's will until we stand before Him and His work is done.

God is dogged in His endurance as well, and wonderfully persistent: He will never, never, never give up on us!

"No amount of falls can really undo us," C. S. Lewis wrote, "if we keep picking ourselves up each time. We shall, of course, be

very muddy and tattered children by the time we reach home. . . .
The only fatal thing is to lose one's temper and give up."

When things go wrong, as they sometimes will,
   When the road you are trudging seems all uphill . . .
When care is pressing you down a bit,
   Rest if you must, but don't you quit. . . .

Many a failure turns about
   When he might have won had he stuck it out;
Don't give up, though the pace seems slow;
   You may well succeed with another blow. . . .

You never can tell how close you are,
   It may be near when it seems afar.
So stick to the fight when you are hardest hit,
   It is when things seem worst that you must not quit.
                              —Author unknown

Postmortem

We die daily. Happy are those
who come to life as well.
—GEORGE MACDONALD

WARM-UP: *2 Kings 13:20–21*

*C*ertain Israelites were burying the body of a dead friend when a bunch of bandits appeared on the horizon. Frightened, they cast the corpse into Elisha's grave and fled.

The moment the body touched the prophet's bones it "came to life" ("lived," to use the author's exact words). The dead man sprang to life, and, I assume, fled from the bandits alongside his friends. (Imagine their surprise!) He must have escaped, because the rabbis claim that after his resuscitation he lived for many years and fathered a large number of children.

Over and over again, Elisha's life and prophecy, and now even his dead bones, established the supremacy of Yahweh and His prophets over the prophets of Baal. In this instance the point being that a dead prophet of Yahweh has more resurrection power than a living prophet of Baal. As Samuel's mother, Hannah, rejoiced in her prayer when she dedicated her son to the service of God: "There is no one . . . like *our* God . . . [who] *makes alive*" (1 Samuel 2:2, 6, emphasis added).

But this story is also a metaphor for the paradox found everywhere in the Bible: that life springs out of death. "Whoever wants to save his life will lose it," Jesus said, "but whoever loses his life for me will save it" (Luke 9:24). Scripture more than once reminds us that if we are to have life we must die.

And there's a second way in which death begets life, for our dying also can bring life to others. Here's the way Paul puts it: "We who are alive are always being given over to death for Jesus' sake, so that his life may be revealed in our mortal body. So then, death is at work in us, but life is at work in you" (2 Corinthians 4:11–12).

Are you in a situation where you must put up with misunderstanding and loss of esteem? Are you beleaguered by a carping, critical spirit in those around you? Do you get little or no credit for the work you do? That's what Paul would call "being given over to death."

The proper response is "the dying of Jesus"; that is, the willing attitude of "dying" daily that continually characterized our Lord. Jesus died every day of His life; the cross was merely the final destination of an entire lifetime of dying. He was willing to be misunderstood and maligned, to take an obscure place, to give up those things that made Him look good in other people's eyes. He met His detractors with kindness and meekness, reacting not in strength, but in weakness.

And if we die with Him, God's gift to us is "the life of Jesus," the most attractive life that ever was lived. His beauty will gradually grow in us and become our beauty as well.

Remember the saying: a picture is worth a thousand words. The portrait you draw of Jesus by your humble, tranquil presence in the face of grievous wrong is worth a spate of words. And some who see the life of Jesus revealed in you will long to enter into that life. Thus, your "mortal flesh" will have brought life to another.

Jesus put the same thought another way: "Unless a kernel of wheat falls to the ground and dies, it remains only a single seed. But if it dies, it produces many seeds" (John 12:24). ❧

Curtain Call

All the world's a stage,
And all the men and women merely players.
—WILLIAM SHAKESPEARE

WARM-UP: *Job 8*

*B*ildad bored in: "If you [Job] were really pure and upright, God would deliver and restore you." Put as a premise: "Goodness and the good life go together."

Bad premise, bad manners, for, as Job wailed, "A despairing man should have the devotion of his friends" (6:14). All Job got, however, was an explanation. Cold comfort to a man who had endured so much pain.

I'm always a bit uneasy around those sincere but all-too-certain folks who can explain everything that comes my way. Their wisdom is proper and theologically familiar, but their explanations, though well-meant, only make me more miserable. I'm more comfortable with those who say, "I'm not sure why you're suffering, but I'll wait here with you and pray." Folks like that are a pure benediction!

Søren Kierkegaard, the Danish philosopher and theologian, once pointed out that human beings are like schoolchildren who want to steal the teacher's answers before a math exam so they don't have to work through the problems. In Job's case, however, there were no answers to steal, at least no earthly answers. His explanation awaited in heaven, where God would supply the reasons behind all he'd suffered. In the meantime he had to rest in the knowledge that there's more to life than he could ever know in this world.

Actually, Bildad was orthodox in his thinking: sin does have its consequences. But in Job's case he was wide of the mark, for Job was a good man. "There is no one on earth like him," said God; "he is blameless and upright, a man who fears God and shuns evil."

No, Bildad's explanation would not do, nor would the explanations of Job's other friends, for they could not know what we know. For in His Word the Lord has provided us with a glimpse behind the curtain—a peek at the drama of the great debate in heaven.

"Does Job fear God for nothing?" Satan asks. "Have you not put a hedge around him and his household and everything he has? You have blessed the work of his hands, so that his flocks and herds are spread throughout the land. But stretch out your hand and strike everything he has, and he will surely curse you to your face." The LORD replies, "Very well, then, everything he has is in your hands" (Job 1:9–12).

Thus, Job found himself the central character in a grand drama, with the entire universe watching, a drama that gives us a glimpse of what God is all about. For it tells us there's something going on that's bigger than we are. That we're part of a larger story, which God is writing for all creation: a love story that will be told through all generations and throughout eternity—how certain men and women clung to God in His absence, in the darkness, when faith seemed like folly, when they were tempted to cut and run.

Will they love Him, though they do not see Him, or hear Him, or feel His loving touch?

I think of Tolkien's *The Lord of the Rings*, the tale of Frodo the hobbit and his friends and their journey to carry the terrible ring to Mordor and destroy it, a journey freighted with grave danger and adversity. The friends reach the borders of Mordor and are climbing the great cliff of Cirith Ungol, a terrible place of darkness and deep shadow, when Frodo at last gives way to terror and discouragement. He's ready to give up and return to the seeming safety of the Shire. "What is the meaning of it all?" he sighs. "Why go on?"

His friend Sam, however, assures Frodo that someday the world will tell his story and put his heroics in perspective: "You know, told by the fireside, or read out of a great big book with red and black letters, years and years afterwards. And people will say: 'Let's hear about Frodo and the Ring!' And they'll say: 'Yes, that's one of my favorite stories. Frodo was very brave, wasn't he, dad?' 'Yes, my boy, the famousest of the hobbits, and that's saying a lot.'"

"That *is* to say a lot," cries Frodo, and he laughs, "a long clear laugh from his heart. Such a sound had not been heard in those places since Sauron came to Middle-earth."

The truth had broken upon Frodo: his suffering was not meaningless after all. It was part of something great and good that would someday touch and grace the entire world, and his response—the response of pure joy—was to laugh.

I, too, must laugh when I think that I, a mere spear-carrier, a minor player, am in the middle of a colossal, cosmic drama, played out before angels and redeemed humanity, a drama in which I am called to suffer and love until the day I die, a love "at which the world grows pale," a love that inspires the hearts of men and angels throughout the universe and through all the ages.

> Then will I strip [my] sleeves and show [my] scars
> Then shall my name be familiar in their mouths as
>   household words...
> This Story shall the good man teach his son,
> From this day on, I shall be remembered.
>   —Shakespeare, *King Henry V*

Learning to Listen

My wife keeps complaining I never
listen to her . . . or something like that.

—Bumper sticker

WARM-UP: *Job 31:35*

*I*t was Renè Descarte, the sixteenth-century philosopher, who said, "I think, therefore I am." Sarah, our granddaughter, says, "You are, therefore I talk."

Some years ago I was sitting in our family room trying to read a *Time* magazine while, at the same time, Sarah was trying to carry on a conversation with me. To my shame I was paying little attention, responding to her comments with an occasional grunt.

Finally, in exasperation, she crawled into my lap and got in my face: "Papa," she shouted, "are you listening to me?"

"Sarah," I confessed, putting down my magazine, "I haven't been listening well. Forgive me. I'll listen to you now."

That's a commitment I want to keep on other occasions as well. I want to learn how to listen.

I want to listen well so that when I finish a conversation others will walk away knowing there's at least one person in this careless world who has some inkling of what they're doing, thinking, and feeling. I want to hear the hushed undertones of their hearts. I want them to know that I care.

Listening, however, doesn't come easy for me. I'm paid to talk—a "wordmonger," to borrow Augustine's apt description of a teacher. So it has come as something of a revelation to me that I can do more with my ears than I can with my mouth.

In her book *Listening to Others,* Joyce Huggett relates her experiences of listening to suffering people. She says they often talk about all she's done for them. "On many occasions," she writes, "I have not 'done' anything. I have 'just listened.' I quickly came to the conclusion that 'just listening' was indeed an effective way of helping others."

This was the help Job's wordy, would-be friends failed to give him. They were "miserable comforters," he complained. "Oh, that I had someone to hear me!" (Job 16:2; 31:35).

Job's friends weren't listening. They didn't hear what he had to say. In fact, he wasn't even sure God was listening.

Job is not alone in his longing. All human beings want to be heard, and listening is one of the best ways in the world to love them. Listening says, "You matter to me; I want to be a friend."

Kenneth Grahame's Badger in *The Wind in the Willows* knew exactly how to do this: "He sat in his arm-chair at the head of the table, and nodded gravely at intervals as the animals told their story; and he did not seem surprised or shocked at anything, and he never said, 'I told you so,' or, 'Just what I always said,' or remarked that they ought to have done so-and-so, or ought not to have done something else. The Mole began to feel very friendly towards him."

Listening is a lost art these days. We don't listen well and we aren't used to being listened to. Most of our words simply fall to the ground.

I have a friend who, when he goes to noisy parties and people ask how he's doing, on occasion has replied quietly, "My business went belly-up this week, the bank foreclosed on my house, my wife left me, and I have terminal cancer." "Wonderful!" one man murmured, as he pumped my friend's hand and moved on. I keep wondering if I've done the same thing to others in other ways.

Here are some things I'm learning about listening:

- When I'm thinking about an answer while others are talking—I'm not listening.

- When I give unsolicited advice—I'm not listening.
- When I suggest they shouldn't feel the way they do—I'm not listening.
- When I apply a quick fix to their problem—I'm not listening.
- When I fail to acknowledge their feelings—I'm not listening.
- When I fidget, glance at my watch, and appear to be rushed—I'm not listening.
- When I fail to maintain eye contact—I'm not listening.
- When I don't ask follow-up questions—I'm not listening.
- When I top their story with a bigger, better story of my own—I'm not listening.
- When they share a difficult experience and I counter with one of my own—I'm not listening.

Listening is hard work and most of us are unwilling to put in the time, and *time* is required. Listening means setting aside our own timetable and tendency to hurry on to our next destination. It means settling into a relaxed, unhurried, leisurely pace. "Only in the ambience of leisure," Eugene Peterson writes, "do persons know they are listened to with absolute seriousness, treated with dignity and importance."

In leisure we regard one another's interests as more important than ours (Philippians 2:3). In leisure we say, "You are more significant than anything I have to do right now. You are the only one who counts, the one for whom I am willing to forget my other obligations, appointments, and meetings. I have time for *you*." In leisure we listen long enough to hear the other person's true heart so that if we do speak, we speak with gentle wisdom.

A leisurely pace, a listening ear, a loving heart, these are the qualities of a good conversationalist. Would that you and I, by God's grace, will acquire them.

A wise old owl lived in an oak;
The more he saw the less he spoke;
The less he spoke the more he heard;
Why can't we all be like that wise old bird?

A final caveat: Even if you listen well, most folks won't make that effort in return. We've all had the experience of leaving a long conversation aware that we know a great deal about the other person, but they know almost nothing about us. "Be patient," Winnie the Pooh says. "If people don't listen, it may be that they have a small piece of fluff in their ear." ❦

Femme Fatale

I've taken my fun where I've found it,
An' now I must pay for my fun.
—RUDYARD KIPLING

WARM-UP: *Proverbs 7*

The wise man has a window on the world. He has seen everything and seen it a hundred times. He spies a young fool sauntering along at dusk, fidgety with the restlessness that sometimes steals upon a man, that odd longing for "he knows not what."

He wanders "in the direction of her house . . . as the dark of night sets in." There's something ominous in those words: you can sense the darkness closing in. A woman is trolling the streets, searching for prey. The street is her killing ground. She is brazen, defiant, shameless, unwilling to abide by her marriage vows.[26]

She entices the young man: she holds him close; she kisses him; she lies to him. "I have come out to meet *you*; I looked for *you* and have found *you*."

She describes her apartment, the feast she has prepared from her portion of the sacrifices, her exotic, perfumed bed, a meal for a famished man.

"My husband is away on a business trip," she says. "We can make love all night long."

"With persuasive words" she leads the young man astray; she seduces him with her sweet talk. He hesitates for a moment, and then "all at once" follows her, not knowing that he is doomed. He is "like a deer stepping into a noose . . . like a bird darting into a snare, little knowing it will cost him his life."

Perhaps the woman's husband shows up unexpectedly and kills the young man. In that culture husbands took such matters into their own hands.

There is, however, another kind of dying: that deathlike state that overwhelms us when we turn from God's will to our own; that awful, empty state in which nothing satisfies or fulfills us.

We gain insight through hindsight, they say, but foresight is the less costly way.

> This is the debt I pay
> Just for one riotous day,
> Years of regret and grief,
> Sorrow without relief...
>
> Slight was the thing I bought,
> Small was the debt I thought,
> Poor was the loan at best—
> God! but the interest!

—Paul Dunbar

The consequences of marital infidelity are vast. The wise man of Proverbs warns that what a man has built with his strength—his family, his business, his reputation—will be torn down. But the greater cost is the toll that adultery takes on his soul. He will have given away his dignity and majesty as a man.

And then there is old age and regret: when a man groans, when his flesh and body are spent, when his body and soul are diminished and dwarfed, when adultery has shriveled his soul.

In his final impotence the man will lament his folly and failure to pay attention to those who taught him wisdom. He will know for himself what T. S. Eliot called "the bitter tastelessness of shadow fruit... the rending pain of reenactment of all that we have done, and been; the sham of motives late revealed, and the awareness of things ill done and done to others' harm." He finds himself on "the brink of utter ruin" (Proverbs 5:14).

Interesting phrase that—on the brink of, not over the edge. God keeps pulling, prodding, calling, wooing us back with His love. He is "forgiving . . . gracious and compassionate, slow to anger and abounding in love" (Nehemiah 9:17). The venal, the sullied, the highly sexed, C. H. Cisson said, are God's "natural prey." ❦

The Man Who Lived Too Long

Better to live well than to live long.
—LUCIUS SENECA (4 B.C–A.D. 65)

WARM-UP: *Isaiah 38:1–5*

*K*ing Hezekiah ruled well for fourteen years. "He removed the high places, smashed the sacred stones and cut down the Asherah poles. He broke into pieces the bronze snake Moses had made, for up to that time the Israelites had been burning incense to it. (It was called Nehushtan.) Hezekiah trusted in the LORD, the God of Israel. There was no one like him among all the kings of Judah, either before him or after him. He held fast to the LORD and did not cease to follow him; he kept the commands the LORD had given Moses" (2 Kings 18:4–6).

But Hezekiah, I'm sad to say, frittered the last years of his life away.[27]

The turning point was Hezekiah's illness, during which the prophet Isaiah came to him with a word from the Lord: "Put your house in order," he said, "because you are going to die" (Isaiah 38:1). Hezekiah had been working on the tapestry of his life, "rolling it up like a weaver," to use his vivid metaphor (38:12). Now the roll had grown large enough—his work was finished—and God was about to cut the cloth from the loom.

The king argued strenuously and tearfully that he could serve God better by living, in answer to which, for some inscrutable reason, the Lord relented and added fifteen years to his life. Unfortunately, Hezekiah did not make the most of his additional years.

When the son of the king of mighty Babylon came with his glittering entourage to pay respects to tiny Judah, Hezekiah, flushed with a sense of his own importance, showed off "his" national treasury while the Babylonians looked on politely, making a mental note to loot it. "I showed them *everything*," Hezekiah boasted to Isaiah. The prophet's response was to inform the king that "everything" was exactly what the Babylonians would seize (39:3–7).

Assured that Judah's doom lay well in the future, however, Hezekiah comforted himself with the self-centered conceit that at least there'd be ease and affluence in his days. He could kick back and indulge himself in careless retirement, which, I believe, is the reason for the foolishness of his final years. For the truth is, we can't just kick back, marking time: we're either growing toward God, or we're going in the other direction.

There's nothing wrong with retiring and setting a slower pace for oneself, but retirement is not the chief end of man. We must grow, mature, serve, minister, mentor, venture ourselves to the end of our days.

You may have heard of John Steven Akhwari, the runner from Tanzania who finished last in the marathon at the 1968 Olympics in Mexico City. No last-place finisher in a marathon ever finished quite so last.

Injured along the way, he hobbled into the stadium over an hour after the last runner had crossed the finish line. All the spectators were gone, the stadium was closed, and crews were preparing for the closing ceremony when Akhwari gathered himself for a final effort and *sprinted* across the line. (I'm told that one of the workers picked up a torn finishing tape and held it across the track so Akhwari could break it.)

When Bud Greenspan, the official filmmaker of the games, asked the weary athlete why he put himself through such pain, Akhwari replied, "Mr. Greenspan, my country did not send me 5,000 miles to start the race. They sent me to *finish* it."

To idle away our last years in self-indulgence and indolence is to rob others and ourselves of the best that is yet to be. Even when "old and gray," we can declare God's "power to the next generation, [His] might to all who are to come" (Psalm 71:18).

There is yet service to be rendered and victories to be won. "Give your fruit before it rots," Richard Rolle said. Finish strong! 🌿

The Tongue of a Learner

I sit down alone.
Only God is here.
In His presence I open,
I read His book;
And what I thus learn,
I speak.
—JOHN WESLEY

WARM-UP: *Isaiah 50:4–5*

*J*esus said we shouldn't worry too much about what to say or how to say it. "At that time you will be given what to say" (Matthew 10:19). That's not to say that God fills our minds with thoughts we've never had before, but rather that He takes from a reservoir of accumulated truth those things that He wants us to say. "Oration follows meditation," the old spiritual masters used to say.

Jesus said to His disciples, "What I tell you in the dark, speak in the daylight; what is whispered in your ear, proclaim from the roofs" (Matthew 10:27). These words are applicable to all of us. Our Lord speaks to us in solitude. There He tells us eternal and infinite secrets. There our eyes begin to see what only He can see; there our ears begin to detect the subtle undertones of His voice.

Listen to the Lord's word to Ezekiel: "'Open your mouth and eat what I give you.' Then Ezekiel looked, and he saw a hand stretched out to him, thrusting a scroll into his hand. Then the Lord said to Ezekiel, 'Son of man, eat what is before you, eat this scroll; then go and speak to the house of Israel.' Then Ezekiel said, 'I opened my mouth, and *he* gave me the scroll to eat'" (Ezekiel 2:8; 3:1–2, italics added).

Isaiah put it this way, speaking of the Servant of the Lord, the Messiah: "The Sovereign LORD has given me an instructed tongue, to know the word that sustains the weary. He wakens me morning by morning, wakens my ear to listen like one being taught" (Isaiah 50:4–5).

What an intriguing image! Every morning God drew near His Servant, calling Him by name, awakening Him, inviting Him to sit at the Father's feet, giving Him His message for the day, preparing Him for each day's duties and demands. Every morning our Lord listened "like one being taught."

That's what enabled Jesus to speak such wise and gracious words to those in need. He knew the source of His wisdom. He said of Himself, "I . . . speak just what the Father has taught me"; I am "a man who has told you the truth that I heard from God"; "These words you hear are not my own; they belong to the Father" (John 8:28, 40; 14:24).

And so it is with us. Every morning our Lord invites us to sit at His feet, to listen like one being taught, to take what words we need for that day. That's how He gives us a wise, instructed tongue. That's how we "know the word that sustains the weary."

Some of the older translations render Isaiah 50:4: "The LORD God has given me the tongue of the *learned*." But the text actually speaks of "the tongue of a *learner*." We must be taught before we can teach others; we must learn before we can ever be "learned." And the more we receive, the more we have to give.

Ambrose, Augustine's mentor, wrote in the fourth century A.D.: "I desire . . . that, in the endeavor to teach, I may be able to learn. For one is the true Master, Who alone has not learnt, what He taught all; but men learn before they teach, and receive from Him what they may hand on to others."

It's through prayerful, thoughtful Bible reading and quiet meditation that our Lord speaks from His depths to ours. It is when we give ourselves time for prayerful contemplation that His heart is revealed and our hearts are exposed. We must listen until we know what He feels, what He wants, what He loves, what He hates. Then we can give that word away.

"Hide yourself in God," George MacDonald said, "and when you rise before men, speak out of that secret place." When we speak out of the secret place, we have the overwhelming authority of God. We are saying again what God has said—nothing more and nothing less.

In our relativistic and subjectivist world the notion of a decisive and final word from God sounds presumptuous. Discovery, dialogue, and debate are more in vogue. But we must never forget that God's word is exactly that—*God's* word. Behind every word we speak lies the infinite power and authority of God Himself, an authority mediated through every utterance. Thus Peter wrote, "If anyone speaks, he should do it *as one speaking the very words of God*" (1 Peter 4:11, italics added). ❧

No Sweat

God always works in tranquility. Fuss and feverishness, anxiety, intensity, intolerance, instability, pessimism and wobble and every kind of worry, these, even on the highest level, are the signs of the self-made and self-acting soul.

—EVELYN UNDERHILL

WARM-UP: *Ezekiel 44:15–18*

The sons of Zadok will "have charge of the altar," God declares as He describes the ideal temple (Ezekiel 40:45–46; 43:19; 48:11). But who was Zadok, and what was so special about his descendants?

Zadok was one of two high priests who served Israel in the early years of King David's reign. Later, when David fled Jerusalem during Absalom's insurrection, Zadok was one of the few courtiers who remained loyal to the king in exile.

He maintained that loyalty. When David was dying and the crown prince Adonijah tried to seize the throne from Solomon, Zadok, along with Benaiah and Nathan the prophet, defended the cause of Solomon and, acting on David's instructions, anointed him king in Gihon. Accordingly, when Solomon established himself on the throne, he appointed Zadok the sole high priest.

Zadok's fame rests squarely on his loyalty to God's plan to bring salvation through David's line. Thus he and his descendants are honored in Ezekiel's vision as true and faithful priests.[28]

Much is said about Zadok's sons in Ezekiel's vision, but the text that captures my attention concerns their apparel. Ezekiel envisions them going about their business, suitably dressed for the occasion: "When they enter the gates of the inner court, they shall wear linen garments; they shall have nothing of wool on them, while they minister at the gates of the inner court, and within. They shall have linen turbans upon their heads, and linen breeches upon their loins; they shall not gird themselves with anything that causes sweat" (Ezekiel 44:17-18 RSV).

This is an allegory, or so it seems to me.[29] We are "a royal priesthood," Peter informs us (1 Peter 2:9). We too serve at God's altar. And as priests we must be appropriately dressed for the occasion: no woolen breeches on our loins, and thus, no sweat. We're meant to be calm, composed believer-priests, exuding an air of tranquility, centers of peace in the midst of the chaos and confusion of our days.

Tranquility is a disposition, a mindset of resting in God for all we have to do, believing that He is at the heart of all our activity and that all the demands upon us are demands upon Him. It is a profound conviction that God is at work while we are at rest, a serene belief that though we're not in control there is a strong, experienced hand at the helm and that everything is working out for the best—for God and ultimately for us.

Tranquility is an unhurried, relaxed lifestyle that grows out of a profound awareness that it is "the LORD [who] builds up Jerusalem" (Psalm 147:2, italics added). It is a confidence that produces in us an immense depth and steadiness in the face of appalling disorder.

"Be full of God's rest," wrote F. B. Meyer. "Let there be no hurry, no fretting. Maintain within your heart the spirit of calm and peace, not fussy, not anxious, nor fretful nor impetuous; refraining your feet from your own paths, your hand from your own devices, refusing to . . . do your own work. It is only when we are fully resolved to act thus, allowing God to originate His own plans and to work in us for their accomplishment that we enter into our inheritance. So shall you build to good and everlasting purpose."

Paul says the very same thing: "Don't worry over anything whatever; whenever you pray tell God every detail of your needs in thankful prayer, and the peace of God, which surpasses human understanding, will keep constant guard over your hearts and minds as they rest in Christ Jesus" (Philippians 4:6–7 PHILLIPS).

No fuss, no frenzy, no sweat. Got your linen britches on? ❦

God Contracted to a Span

'Twas much that man
was made like God before,
But that God should be made like man—
much more.

—JOHN DONNE

WARM-UP: *Micah 4:6–8; Luke 2:8–20*

*M*icah predicted that the announcement of Messiah's birth would be delivered at Migdol-Eder ("The Watch Tower of the Flock"), traditionally identified as the Shepherd's Field a few thousand yards north of Bethlehem.

The heavenly messenger passed by Jerusalem, where the scholars and clergy of the day were ensconced. He passed by the Herodium, Herod's hilltop villa near Bethlehem. He bypassed all the elite and appeared instead to a group of shepherds squatting around a campfire, telling lies, passing a wineskin and passing the long, cold night.

Back then no one would have thought that God would be interested in shepherds, or that shepherds would be interested in God. Shepherds were notoriously irreligious and unbothered with spiritual things. They were more like Owyhee County buckaroos, the old-time cowboys who work the desert near our home in Boise, than the sanitized sheepherders we associate with the story these days. Ranked by the rabbis with prostitutes and other "habitual sinners," shepherds were outcasts, rejects, pariahs, barred from synagogue and polite society. One rabbi declared: "In the whole world you will find no occupation more despised than the shepherd."[30] Shepherds assumed that God would never take a liking to the likes of them, and feared Him in the worst possible way.

But God never wastes His words, and He speaks only to those who want to hear what He has to say. He knew that these shepherds, underneath their seeming indifference and ever-hardening crust, were incurably religious men who, in desperation, quietly longed for God.

Such longing haunts all of us, no matter how hard and tough we try to be. Sooner or later we run out of something essential—love, money, time, or life. Isolation, loneliness, impotence, and fear of death lead us to acknowledge our need for a Savior. But—where can we find Him?

The angel's words were simple and direct: "Today in the city of David there has been born for you a Savior, who is Christ the Lord. And this will be a sign for you: you will find a baby wrapped in cloths, and lying in a manger" (Luke 2:11–12 NASB).

A Savior "born for *you*." This was the good news that brought the shepherds great joy! And what was the sign? They would find Him "in a manger"—in a feed trough.

And so the shepherds hurried off in search of their Savior. They didn't bother to look in Herod's villa, for there were no feed troughs up there. They skirted the resorts, the spas, the lodges of the rich and famous and went looking instead for a feedlot, a stockyard, or one of the damp and dirty caves into which they drove their own flocks at night. And there, in the mud and dung, where Joseph and Mary had crept to find shelter from the cold, they found a helpless infant, with unfocused eyes and uncontrolled limbs, needing to be cuddled and cared for, made terribly vulnerable, humble, and exceedingly small. The God-baby in the straw. God in a form no one could possibly fear.

The feed trough was no afterthought. All along God has been doing His best to get next to us, humbling Himself to reach out to us. But nothing can match what happened that night in that

Bethlehem cave. There a child was born among "the sweet breath and steaming dung of beasts and nothing is ever the same again . . . Once [we] have seen him in a stable, [we] can never be sure where he will appear, or to what lengths he will go or to what ludicrous depths of self-humiliation he will descend in his wild pursuit of man."[31]

"Wild pursuit" indeed! Which is Micah's point exactly: "In that day," declares the LORD, "I will . . . gather the *outcasts*" (Micah 4:6 NASB, italics added). ❦

One Good Man

We mostly spend [our] lives conjugating three verbs: to Want, to Have, and to Do. Craving, clutching, and fussing, on the material, political, social, emotional, intellectual—even on the religious—plane, we are kept in perpetual unrest: forgetting that none of these verbs have any ultimate significance, except so far as they are transcended by and included in, the fundamental verb, to Be: and that Being, not wanting, having and doing, is the essence of a spiritual life.

—EVELYN UNDERHILL

WARM-UP: *Matthew 1:18–25*

*J*oseph, the husband of Mary, is a dim figure in the background of the Christmas drama. He drops offstage almost immediately and is never heard of again. And he is known for one thing alone: he was "a righteous [good] man" (1:19).

Joseph was a man in whom mercy triumphed over justice. When he discovered that Mary was pregnant, though he could have shamed her and saved himself a good deal of embarrassment, he chose to shield her from disgrace. (A good man would never humiliate anyone, especially the woman he loves.)

Joseph was a man who, though he could not quite grasp the immensity of what was going on around him, was quick to respond to what he perceived to be the will of God.

Joseph was a man whose mercy translated into a strong, enduring love for Mary that transcended self-interest; a man who left everything—home, country, and business—and fled to Egypt to save Mary and the baby Jesus.

In our Scripture record, Joseph never utters a word—not one word, not one syllable, not one sound—yet he speaks to us today.

Where are those Joseph-men today? Men who are authentically and transparently good? Why are they so few? Good old boys come and go, but good men are much harder to find.

Finding work is more highly valued than being good these days, or so it seems to me. We hustle through life in the hope that if we do something long enough, well enough, and make enough money we'll be worth something someday. That's why when we meet an individual for the first time, we usually ask, "What do you do?" For what a person *does* is what matters most, or so we seem to believe. The better question is the one we ask small children, "When you grow up, what do you want to *be*?"

Most of us want to *be* something, but first we have to *do*: we have a career to manage, money to make, a ministry to carry out— miles to go and promises to keep. That's our besetting, beguiling sin: always chasing after that elusive "something more." One more deal to make, one more hill to climb, one more challenge to overcome, one more program to enact. But as Thoreau would warn us, such preoccupation only leads to a life of quiet desperation, be it healthy, wealthy, or otherwise.

The better course is to "seek first his [God's] kingdom and his righteousness," as Jesus said, for one quest leads inexorably to the other (Matthew 6:33).

When we design our days to make time for God, we reflect each day a little more of His righteousness. And the time to begin is right now. "How we spend our days is how we spend our hours," says Annie Dillard. "What we do with *this* hour is what we are doing." ❧

Pulling an Eddie

I will tell you. Get up, and do something
the Master tells you; so make yourself
his disciple at once.
—GEORGE MACDONALD

WARM-UP: *Matthew 14:22–33*

Certain sports figures have forever endeared themselves to us. One is British ski jumper Eddie "the Eagle" Edwards, who competed in the 1988 Winter Olympics in Calgary and whose lunacy captured our hearts.

Who can forget the nationally televised interview in which he was asked what he hoped to accomplish in the Olympics. Eddie replied, "As a ski jumper, I hope to get from first to last as soon as I can! Uh, I mean. . . ." (Edwards actually finished fifty-fifth in a field of fifty-six jumpers. The fifty-sixth jumper was disqualified.)

Millions of viewers watched with their hearts in their mouths as Eddie careened down the 90-meter hill and windmilled into space. I'm told that Eddie's birthday, December 5, is still celebrated by casualty departments around the world.

Eddie has his very own entry in the *Oxford Book of Words and Phrases,* where "Pulling an Eddie" is defined as "doing something extremely badly, and doing it in the most embarrassing manner possible."

Nevertheless, Eddie went for it—that's the important thing— and actually got better, competing in later years with greater ability. Which leads me to conclude that doing extremely badly can be one of the ways we grow. Ask Peter, who once tried to walk on water.

The story, as Matthew tells it, takes place on the Sea of Galilee one stormy night. The disciples were in their fishing boats, rowing against a stiff wind, when Jesus walked by them—on the water!

Mark, in his parallel account, tells us that Jesus intended to "pass them by," using a verb that the Greek version of the Old Testament uses for a "theophany," an occasion when God revealed Himself to certain men and women and called them to a new level of accomplishment.

According to the story, the disciples were at first frightened, thinking they were seeing an apparition. Then, when assured it was Jesus, Peter cried out, "Lord, if it's you, tell me to come to you on the water" (Matthew 14:28).

Peter could have stayed in the boat, safe from wind and waves. But God had placed in Peter, as He has placed in us, a hunger for high adventure. So when Jesus called out to Peter: "Come!" Peter leaped out of the boat and began to walk toward Jesus on the crests of the waves.

But when he realized what he was actually doing, Peter panicked and began to sink. "Lord, save me!" he cried out. Immediately Jesus reached out, took his hand, pulled him out of the water, and they walked together to the boat.

Did Peter do extremely badly? Indeed. Did he do it in the most embarrassing manner possible? Absolutely. But—and here's the point—*Peter walked on water*, the only disciple ever to do so. And he never forgot the feeling, or the hand that lifted him out of his failure and sustained him as he walked again.

So, I ask you, what is God calling *you* to do this year? You say, "I'm just an ordinary person. My circumstances are restricted; my conditions are commonplace. What can I do? And how can I know what God wants me to do or to be?"

He will let you know. It may be to follow your heart's desire for deeper intimacy with God and personal holiness. It may be to fulfill your longing to teach a child, or to share your faith with a neighbor. It may be to inveigh against some sin in you that you can hardly stand to look at, or to think about—a perverse thing that has defeated you again and again. It may be a godly choice that will result in cruel ridicule, or an act so far beyond you that it seems ridiculous to try.

That drawing in your soul, that dawning of hope is the voice of God Himself telling you to come. Get out of your boat and walk—even if at first you don't succeed. As a friend of mine says, "If a thing is worth doing, it's worth doing badly." ❧

Holy Chance

I was on my way to the fields when I saw Him carrying
 His cross;
and multitudes were following Him.
Then I too walked beside Him.
His burden stopped Him many a time,
for His body was exhausted.
Then a Roman soldier approached me, saying,
"Come, you are strong and firm built; carry the cross of
 this man."

—KAHLIL GIBRAN

WARM-UP: *Mark 15:21*

*I*t was a morning like any other morning as Simon of Cyrene made his way through the crowded streets of Jerusalem. It was Passover, always a hectic time in the city, and he was focusing on his own business, when he came upon a Roman procession and a man dragging the beam of cross. This was a common sight in Simon's day, for crucifixion was Rome's favorite form of capital punishment.

Simon would have "passed by," Mark says, not wanting to be involved in this ugly scene. But the cross-bearing man stumbled, unable to carry his load, and the soldiers, wanting to get on with their business, pulled Simon out of the crowd and forced him to carry the heavy wooden beam.[32]

Bad luck for Simon, we say. No, "all luck is holy," as Charles Williams says, for this random pick was God's election for Simon.

Simon's story occurs in each of the Synoptic Gospels (Matthew 27; Mark 15; Luke 23), so it must have been important to the writers. But why is this "nobody" so duly noted?

Mark gives us a clue: In his account he calls Simon "the father of Alexander and Rufus," and does so without explanation, leading us to believe that his readers in Rome were acquainted with these two young men.[33]

Paul, likewise, writing to the same church, mentions "Rufus, chosen in the Lord, and his mother, who has been a mother to me, too" (Romans 16:13). This is the same Rufus of whom Mark wrote, so he must have been well-known among the Christians in Rome. Paul's affectionate reference to Rufus's mother as "his mother and mine" also suggests that Paul was a friend of the family and a frequent guest in their home.

Simon is not mentioned in Paul's letter, presumably because he died before Paul wrote to the church at Rome. As for Alexander, tradition says that he was an early Christian martyr and that at the time Paul wrote, he, too, had already gone home to God. (It's worth noting that an ossuary containing the bones of "Alexander, son of Simon, of Cyrene" has been found in Jerusalem. Also, Luke reports that on the day of Pentecost the apostles proclaimed the Gospel to "residents of Mesopotamia, Judea and Cappadocia, Pontus and Asia, Phrygia and Pamphylia, Egypt *and the parts of Libya near Cyrene*" (Acts 2:9–10, italics added).)

All of these subtle clues lead me to believe that somewhere along the Via Dolorosa, or at the foot of the cross, or at Pentecost, Simon *believed*.

The poet Kahlil Gibran makes the same assumption, putting these words in Simon's mouth: "I was filled with wonder. Now, the cross I carried has become *my* cross. Should they say to me again, 'Carry the cross of this man,' I would carry it till my road ended at the grave . . ."

> This happened many years ago;
> and still whenever I follow the furrow in the field,
> and in that drowsy moment before sleep,
> I think always of that Beloved Man.

Simon went home to Cyrene a follower of Jesus, or so I believe, and became the first herald of the Gospel to Africa. His wife and sons also became followers of Christ and important leaders in the early church. One son, Alexander, died as a Christian martyr; the other, Rufus, was known and beloved as "a choice servant of the Lord." And after Simon's death, his widow tenderly mothered the homeless, motherless apostle Paul and greatly encouraged him. All of this resulted because of Simon's "chance" encounter.

I recall a day and a freeway in California on which I picked up a bearded, pony-tailed hitchhiker, a philosophy student from the University of California at Berkeley. As we chatted, I realized that this was a young man who thought deeply about life and I asked him if he had any interest in spiritual things.

"Friend," he said, turning in his seat, "I've been looking for God all my life. Can you tell me how to know God?"

Chance encounter? Holy chance, I say. ❧

Exactly Right

I look at the situation before me as if it
were exactly right for me.
—MADAM GUYON

WARM-UP: *Luke 1:26–38*

The angel said to Mary, "You have found favor with God. You will be with child and give birth to a son" (Luke 1:30–31). The angelic announcement, which brings us such joy, brought unspeakable heartache to Mary.

From the beginning, rumors swirled around her character. The Pharisaic brush-off, "[At least] we are not illegitimate children" (John 8:41), is perpetuated in the ancient Talmud, a collection of Rabbinic writings that describes Jesus as "the illegitimate son of Mary." And then there was Mary's husband-to-be, Joseph, and his impetuous decision to "put her away"; the sudden departure for Bethlehem in the last days of her pregnancy; the unassisted birth in a cold, filthy cave; the perilous flight to escape Herod's fury—all the beginning of sorrows that culminated at the foot of the cross when a sword, as Simon predicted, was thrust to the hilt into Mary's soul.

But Mary knew that her lot was ordained by God, and she humbly accepted His will: "I am the Lord's servant. May it be to me as you have said" (Luke 1:38). We must not forget her heartache, and we must not fail to learn her words.

We must learn them in the realities of life that are thrust upon us: in the care of an aging, ill-tempered parent, or a disagreeable ADHD child; in a trying and tiresome marriage where nothing works and nothing seems to matter; in the humbling of physical disablement or disfigurement; in the burden of prolonged pain and suffering; in the cramping restrictions of mindless and meaningless work; in the emptiness of a lonely and loveless existence; in the losses and limitations that accompany old age.

If we plan to move into intimacy with Jesus, we must abandon our whole existence, offering it up to Him. We must believe that every circumstance of our life—every moment as well as the course of our entire life, anything and everything that happens to us—has come to us by God's will and by His permission and is exactly what we need.

The only way to learn Mary's words is to know that God's will is "good, acceptable and perfect," and to accept day by day the conditions and circumstances He permits; to lay down our will and patiently submit to His will as it is presented to us day by day in the form of the people with whom we have to live and work, and in the things that keep happening to us.

Jeanne Guyon, a seventeenth-century woman, learned Mary's words. At age sixteen, Jeanne was forced into an arranged marriage with an invalid forty years older than she. She found her marriage to be a place of utter humiliation. Her husband was an angry melancholic. Her mother-in-law was a merciless critic. Even her servant girl despised her. Despite her best attempts at devotion to her husband and family, Madame Guyon found herself subject to relentless criticism and hostility.

Forbidden by her husband to go to church, she sought God in His Word and worshiped Him in secret. Alone with God, she learned that each situation before her was, as she put it, "exactly right," and thus, despite her dreary circumstances, she was "perfectly fine—within the safe hands of God."[34]

She writes, "Here is a true spiritual principle that the Lord will not deny: God gives us the cross and the cross gives us God. . . . Abandonment [to His cross] is the key to the inward spiritual life. It is the key to fathomless depths."[35]

"But," you say, "I'm a woman or a man of action. I make things happen. This counsel is much too passive for me." Consider Mary, the mother of our Lord: through her "passivity," God brought forth our salvation.

> This, then, is our prayer, "May it be to me as you have said."
> I said, "I will accept the breaking sorrow
> Which God tomorrow
> Will to me explain."
> Then did the turmoil deep within me cease.
> Not vain the word: vain, vain;
> For in acceptance lieth peace.
>
> —Amy Carmichael

Simeon's Farewell

Let the Infant, the still unspeaking and unspoken Word,
Grant Israel's consolation
To one who has eighty years and no tomorrow.
—T. S. ELIOT, "A SONG FOR SIMEON"

WARM-UP: *Luke 2:25–35*

*S*imeon was a venerable old saint who had long waited "the comforting of Israel" (cf. Isaiah 40:1). The Holy Spirit had revealed to him "that he would not die before he had seen the Lord's Christ" (Luke 2:26).

"By chance," some would erringly say, Simeon arrived at the temple when Mary and Joseph brought the infant Jesus "to present him to the Lord," as the Law commanded. Seeing the child, Simeon took Him from His mother, cradled Him in his arms, and began to sing:

> "Sovereign Lord, as you have promised,
>   you now dismiss your servant in peace.
> For my eyes have seen your salvation,
>   which you have prepared in the sight of all people,
> A light for revelation to the Gentiles
>   and for glory to your people Israel" (Luke 2:29–32).[36]

Much of what Simeon sang about Jesus came from the prophet Isaiah, who promised that *all the ends of the earth* will see the salvation of our God" (Isaiah 52:10, italics added). This infant would bring glory to Israel and revelation to the Gentiles spread around the world.

This was surely a moment of great joy for Mary. All mothers know that their children are special, but for Mary this was a public ratification of what she already knew: that her son's kingdom would "have no end" (Luke 1:33 NASB).[37]

But Simeon then states a hard fact. Though the Child was appointed for the "rise of many" (Luke 2:34 NASB), many would fall—trip over—Him and curse Him in the darkness. He would be slandered, rejected, and killed, and Mary herself would suffer excruciating pain.

Simeon's words reinforce the bittersweet quality of the nativity: the story delights us, but we know that the birth of this child will lead to suffering—as do, in fact, all births. Perhaps that's why we old folks are strangely moved when we look at snapshots of happy parents cradling a newborn baby, for we know that their child will surely suffer and that a sword will pierce their own souls as well. I've been around too long and have seen too much to believe otherwise.

How often have I listened to the stories of old friends and thought back to our youthful naiveté. Little did we know what sufferings we would endure.

I think of a childhood friend whose wife was murdered in a savage invasion of their home, while he was left confined to a wheelchair. Two other friends have challenged children; others have lost their children or seen them damaged in tragic ways. One friend's wife was injured in an accident from which she never fully recovered; others have suffered multiple losses through disease, death, or divorce. In fact, I can think of no childhood friend who has not suffered in a significant way, recalling George Herbert's poignant words, "I cried when I was born and every day shows why."

"In the world you will have tribulation," Jesus said. "But," He continued, "be of good cheer." And I must say that, despite their challenges, my friends are of good cheer. They sorrow—Christianity is not Stoicism; there's no virtue in the stiff upper lip—but they do not sorrow as those who have no hope, for they have learned that we all share in Jesus' sufferings. For if nothing else, the Incarnation tells us that at the center of our life is One who has been broken—who, from the cradle to the cross, has been one with us in our pain and loss.

Dorothy Sayers puts it this way: "For whatever reason God chose to make man as he is—limited and suffering and subject to sorrows and death—He had the honesty and courage to take His own medicine. Whatever the game He is playing with His creation, He has kept His own rules and played fair. He can exact nothing from man that He has not exacted from Himself. He has Himself gone through the whole of human experience—the humiliation of the manger, the trivial irritations of family life, the cramping restrictions of hard work and lack of money, the worst horrors of pain and humiliation, defeat, despair, and death."[38]

Does God promise that we will not feel pain? Not in this life. Does He feel our pain? The Incarnation is the final, irrefutable proof that He does. We can cast our care upon Him knowing that our sufferings matter to Him, that He cares, and sometimes that's all we need to know.

There is great relief in laying our burden down, even briefly, in the presence of someone who understands and cares. Author Margaret Guenther tells of a Scottish pediatrician who comforted her hurt and frightened child, not with medicine, but with a great, enveloping bear hug and the words, "Och, poor wee bairn!"

"The poor wee bairn stopped crying at once," Mrs. Guenther said, "for she realized that another understood her pain and did not seek to minimize it."

Thus Jesus comforts our broken hearts. "Blessed are those who mourn, for they *will* be comforted" (Matthew 5:4, italics added). 🖋

Growing Old with God

To know how to grow old is the masterwork of wisdom and
one of the most difficult chapters in the great art of living.
—Henri Amiel

WARM-UP: *Luke 2:36–38*

Anna was old—waiting for "the death wind," as T. S. Eliot would say. She had been married for seven years, but then her husband died and she was a widow until she was eighty-four. Anna never missed a service at the temple, worshiping night and day, fasting and praying.

Anna had grown old with God, the alternative of which is to grow old *without* him.

Growing old, as they say, is not for sissies. Aging is often accompanied and overclouded by both physical and personal losses—separation and bereavement, physical and mental decline. These blows can fall on us at any time, but they seem to fall heaviest in our latter years. None of us can shield ourselves from these difficulties or physical infirmities, but we can do our best to ensure that our senior years will be happy and productive, years of growth in grace and beauty rather than years of boredom and futility. The secret is developing the inward life of the soul.

Age breaks down our strength and energy, but it also strips us of our busyness so we have more time to develop intimacy with God. Far from frustrating God's best in us, the weakness and limitations of age enable us to grow to full maturity. The culmination of the process is body and spirit united—one in loving God and others. Without the limitations of old age we might never make the most of our lives.

I recall a man saying to me that long years of weakness and failing health had made his life worth living. "How awful it would have been if, instead of getting old, I'd been extinguished in middle age without learning what God has to offer."

Our senior years can be viewed as a pleasantly useless era where we qualify for Social Security, AARP, and senior discounts and when we have a lot of free time to play golf, or those years can be anticipated as a time of great usefulness to God. The opportunities are limited only by our imagination and our physical stamina. We can serve as mentors and conservators of wisdom and virtue, the essential role elders play in society and in the church—grand old men and women who point out the ancient paths and show young believers how to walk them. "Stand at the crossroads and look; ask for the ancient paths, ask where the good way is, and walk in it, and you will find rest for your souls" (Jeremiah 6:16).

Consider the power of an ordinary life lived with an awareness of God's presence, seeing Him in everything and doing all things for Him. Teresa of Avila found God in her kitchen, walking among the pots and pans. Brother Lawrence, the author of *Practicing the Presence of God*, saw God in his mundane tasks in a monastic scullery. This is the mark of the mature soul: quietly, humbly going about his or her homely tasks, living in joy and leaving behind the sweet fragrance of Jesus' love.

And by God's grace, we can grow sweeter as the days go by, easier to live with, more delightful to be around.

Izaak Walton wrote of an old companion: "How comforting it is to see a cheerful and contented old age . . . after being tempest-tossed through life, safely moored in a snug and quiet harbor in the evening of his days! His happiness . . . was independent of external circumstances, for he had that inexhaustible good nature which is the most precious gift of Heaven, spreading itself like oil over the troubled sea of thought, and keeping the mind smooth and equable in the roughest weather." This is the mind that is stayed on God.

Even when our journey leads into illness and weakness and we're confined to our homes and then our beds, our years of fruitful activity are not over. Like Anna, we can worship and pray night and day. Prayer is the special privilege of infirmity and, in the end, perhaps its greatest contribution.

> The soul's dark cottage, batter'd and decay'd,
> Lets in new light through chinks that Time has made;
> Stronger by weakness, wiser, men become
> As they draw near their eternal home.
> —Edmund Waller (1606–1687)

And we can love. Love remains our last and best gift to God and to others. As St. John of the Cross wrote in good old age, "Now I guard no flock, nor have I any office. Now my work is in loving alone" (*A Spiritual Canticle*).

Prayer and love. These are the mighty works of the elderly.

And then, on ahead, awaits the resurrection of our ruined old bodies—what ancient spiritual writers called *athanasias pharmakon* (the medicine of immortality)—God's cure for all that ails us. This is God's loving purpose for us beyond all earthly existence, "that when this mildew age has dried away, our hearts will beat again as young and strong and gay" (George MacDonald).

Some years ago, in a small chapel in Oxford, England, I came across this prayer of a seventeenth-century nun. In her godly wisdom, she sums up the aging attitude I would have—and would wish for you:

> Keep me from the fatal habit of thinking that I must say something on every subject and on every occasion.
> Release me from craving to straighten out everybody's affairs. With my vast store of wisdom, it seems a pity not

to use it all, but you know, Lord, that I want a few friends at the end.

Keep my mind free from the recital of endless details; give me wings to get to the point.

Seal my lips on my aches and pains. They are increasing, and love of rehearsing them is becoming sweeter as the years go by. I dare not ask for grace enough to enjoy the tales of others' pains, but help me to endure them with patience.

I dare not ask for improved memory, but for a growing humility when my memory seems to clash with the memories of others.

Teach me the glorious lesson that occasionally I may be mistaken. Keep me reasonably sweet; I do not want to be a saint—some of them are so hard to live with—but a sour old person is one of the crowning works of the devil.

Give me the ability to see good things in unexpected people. And give me, Lord, the grace to tell them so. Amen. ❦

A Place to Grow

Bloom where you're planted.
—Folk saying

WARM-UP: *Luke 2: 39–52*

We know nothing about Jesus' activity during the first twenty-nine years of His life, apart from Luke's brief notice in the second chapter of his gospel. There are a number of so-called "gospels" from the second century that recount fantastic tales of miracles Jesus performed during this period, but none of this material is authentic. It was clearly fictitious, heretical in purpose, and was disregarded by early Christians.

So what was Jesus doing during this period of obscurity?

Growing! That's what He was doing.

Luke brackets the temple incident with two descriptions of Jesus' growth and development: "And the child *grew* and became strong; he was filled with wisdom, and the grace of God was upon him. . . . And Jesus *grew* in wisdom and stature, and in favor [grace] with God and men" (Luke 2:40, 52, italics added). Both verses stress the fact that Jesus was *growing*.

Some of the earlier translations, such as the KJV, use the phrase "strong in spirit" in verse 40 ("the child grew, and waxed strong in spirit"). Though this is probably a scribal note, it may reflect the original sense of the text.

The word "stature" in Luke 2:52 most likely refers to *moral* stature rather than physical size. It's the word Paul uses in Ephesians 4:13 to refer to our growth in likeness to Christ: "until we . . . become mature, attaining to the whole measure [stature] of the fullness of Christ."

Our Lord had an infinite job to do and yet He was not pressured by the passage of time. He was wholly content to live in obscurity—and grow.

Seventeen years after His appearance in the temple, Jesus surfaced during John the Baptist's ministry and joined the believing remnant by baptism. As He emerged from the water, His Father said from heaven: "You are my Son, whom I love; with you I am well pleased" (Luke 3:22).

What had Jesus been doing during the past twenty-nine years that merited such unqualified acceptance? He had not performed any miracles; He had not preached a single sermon; He had not cleansed one leper. He had, in fact, done none of the things we normally associate with greatness. He was merely growing in grace—and thus found "favor with God" (2:52).

Nazareth and the hidden years are the secret of Jesus' usefulness. In that hidden place He was sharpened and shaped. There He learned to know His Father and His Father's will. There He learned obedience.

Jesus never got away from His need for seclusion. When His public ministry began and people were gathering in large numbers, clamoring for His presence, He frequently walked away. Luke reports that as news of Jesus' ministry spread, "crowds of people came to hear him and to be healed of their sicknesses. But Jesus often withdrew to lonely places and prayed" (Luke 5:15–16).

It wasn't that He had an aversion to people, even people *en masse*. He had come to save them. It was a matter of maintaining a safe place. He knew He needed quiet times for soul-making.

It's in the quiet, lonely, secret places that we're shaped and molded and made into men and women God can use.

Perhaps you've been displaced or sidelined. Perhaps you're subject to the cramping constrictions of age, illness, a difficult child, or an uncooperative spouse. Take heart. Your limited place can never limit you. Embrace it as a place to grow, a place to deepen and sweeten your relationship with God. Don't worry about being useful. God will reward you in due time.

Charles de Foucauld, a nineteenth-century missionary to North Africa, wrote, "We do good to others, not in the measure of our words or actions, but in the measure of what we are.... He who would be useful to souls must first labor with all strength and continuously at the task of... personal sanctification."

Three examples come to mind: an elderly couple living quietly out of the mainstream, but still growing—rising up every morning and moving into God's presence, studying, pondering, praying over God's Word. Their apartment is just another place to grow. When I'm around them, I feel like taking off my shoes; I'm on holy ground.

Then there's a friend who left an active ministry and took a job clearing tables in an institutional dining room. Like Brother Lawrence, the Carmelite lay brother, he's daily on the job, blending work with prayer. His ordinary, everyday kitchen is just another place to grow.

And finally there is the apostle Paul: restrained in Rome in the Mamertine Prison; unable to preach, teach, or evangelize; under sentence of death; at the end of the line. Yet he writes to Timothy: "When you come, bring... my scrolls, especially the *parchments* [his Bible]" (2 Timothy 4:13, italics added). Paul's cell was just another place to grow. 🌿

The Weightier Matters of the Law

Get rid of everything in your wardrobe that is not white. Stop sleeping on a soft pillow. Sell your musical instruments and stop eating white bread. You cannot take warm baths, or shave off your beard. To shave is to lie against Him who created us because it is an attempt to improve upon His work.

—FROM A SECOND-CENTURY CATECHISM

WARM-UP: *Luke 7:36–50*

The genius of legalism is that it misses the point. Legalists "go beyond what is written," to use Paul's expression (1 Corinthians 4:6), then give their additions and extra-biblical prohibitions the authority of inspired Scripture.

Consider Simon, for example, who invited Jesus to his house for lunch. Simon was a rigid, rule-keeping Pharisee and thus gave his hands a rigorous scrubbing as the "tradition of the elders" (the Jewish rabbis) prescribed (cf. Mark 7:3–5). He washed his cups and saucers, pots and pans with nervous scrupulosity. He observed every Pharisaic directive—but he neglected love, the weightier matter of the law. That's what Jesus meant when He said to the Pharisees, "You strain out a gnat but swallow a camel" (Matthew 23:24).

Here's a selection from the Mishnah, a written collection of some of the earliest oral interpretations of the Law by the rabbis. This paragraph is called *Yadaim* ("Hands"):

> To render the hands clean a quarter-log or more of water must be poured over the hands for one person or even for two;

a half log or more suffices for three persons or for four; one log or more [suffices] for five or for ten or for a hundred. R. Jose says: Provided that for the last among them there remains not less than a quarter-log. More [water] may be added to the second [water that is poured over the hands], but more may not be added to the first.... The custom was to give the hands a double rinsing; if for the second rinsing the remaining water was not enough to reach the wrist, more water may be added to the residue.... The water may be poured over the hands out of any vessel, even from vessels made from cattle-dung or vessels of stone or vessels of [unbaked] clay. It may not be poured over the hands out of the sides of [broken] vessels or out of the flanks of a ladling-jar, nor may a man pour it over his fellow's hands out of his cupped hands, for they may not draw the water or mix the ashes or sprinkle the Sin-offering water, or pour [water] over the hands, save only in a vessel; and only vessels that have a tightly stopped-up cover afford protection against uncleanness and only vessels afford protection against uncleanness present in earthenware vessels. If water was [so polluted that it was] unfit for cattle to drink, if it was in vessels it is invalid [for the washing of hands], but if it was on the ground it is valid. If ink, gum, or copperas fell therein and its color was changed, it becomes invalid. If a man did any act of work therewith, or if he soaked his bread therein, it becomes invalid. Simeon of Teman says: If it was his intention to soak it in other water but it fell in this water, the water remains valid.

There was a woman at Simon's house that day who knew nothing of these rules. She did, however, know how to love: "She brought an alabaster jar of perfume, and as she stood behind [Jesus] at his feet weeping, she began to wet his feet with her tears" (Luke 7:37-38).

"Simon," Jesus said, "you did not give me any water for my feet, but she wet my feet with her tears and wiped them with her hair. You did not give me a kiss, but this woman, from the time I entered, has not stopped kissing my feet. You did not put oil on my head, but she has poured perfume on my feet.... for *she loved much*" (Luke 7:44–47, italics added).

Much love. That is the measure of true holiness.

Simon's rules go straight to the heart of the issue. Legalism makes secondary things primary and primary things secondary; it subordinates love to regulations and rigmarole, and thus misses the heart of the Gospel and the great heart of God.

God does draw fine lines. In our fallen state, He must tell us what behaviors are truly loving. But all of God's lines lead to unconditional love. "The commandments, 'Do not commit adultery,' 'Do not murder,' 'Do not steal,' 'Do not covet,' and whatever other commandment there may be, are summed up in this one rule," says Paul. "Love your neighbor as yourself" (Romans 13:9). Love is the point of the Word.

One story makes this argument far better than I. It comes from an old volume I found in a dusty bin at a garage sale. The old Scotsman, George MacDonald, tells the story in a way that touches me in ways I cannot express. I leave it with you for your consideration.

"You smoke, don't you, Rogers?" I said.

"Well, sir, I can't deny it. It's not much I spend on baccay, anyhow. Is it, dame?"

"No, that it bean't," answered his wife.

"You don't think there's any harm in smoking a pipe, sir?"

"Not the least," I answered, with emphasis.

"You see, sir," he went on, not giving me time to prove how far I was from thinking there was any harm in it, "you see, sir, sailors learns many ways they might be better without. I used to take my pan o' grog with the rest of them; but I give that up quite, 'cause as how I don't want it now."

"Cause as how," interrupted his wife, "you spend the money on tea for me, instead. You wicked old man to tell stories!"

"Well, I takes my share of the tea, old woman, and I'm sure it's a deal better for me. But, to tell the truth, sir, I was a little troubled in my mind about the baccay, not knowing whether I ought to have it or not. For you see, the parson that's gone didn't like it, as I could tell when he came in at the door and me a-smokin'. Not as he said anything; for, ye see, I was an old man, and I daresay that kep him quiet. But I did hear him blow up a young chap i' the village he came upon with a pipe in his mouth. He did give him a thunderin' broadside, to be sure! So I was in two minds whether I ought to be on with my pipe or not."

"And how did you settle the question, Rogers?"

"Why, I followed my own, old chart, sir."

"Quite right. One mustn't mind too much what other people think."

"That's not exactly what I mean, sir."

"What do you mean then? I should like to know."

"Well, sir, I mean that I said to myself, 'Now, Old Rogers, what do you think the Lord would say about this here baccay business?'"

"And what did you think He would say?"

"Why, sir, I thought He would say, 'Old Rogers, have yer baccay; only mind ye don't grumble when you 'ain't got none.'" 🌿

Holy Dying

From lightning and tempest; from earthquake, fire, and flood; from plague, pestilence, and famine . . . from oppression, conspiracy, and rebellion; from violence, battle, and murder; and from dying suddenly and unprepared, Good Lord, deliver us.

—THE GREAT LITANY

WARM-UP: *Luke 12:16–21*

*P*ity the poet Aeschylus, who survived the battles of Marathon, Artemisium, Salamis, and Platæa and was resting outside his home in Sicily one day when an eagle hovering overhead mistook his bald head for a stone and dropped a tortoise on it to break its shell. He broke instead the poor man's skull.

Lightning, tempest, earthquake, fire, flood, plague, pestilence, famine, oppression, conspiracy, rebellion, violence, battle, and murder can take us suddenly, as The Great Litany, an ancient prayer, puts it. "From dying unprepared, Good Lord, deliver us."

We don't think much about death these days—at least not like they did in earlier times when folks were more comfortable with the subject. In that era, churches were surrounded by cemeteries and filled with sepulchers—somber and constant reminders that one's body would one day lie under a slab. Additionally there was a good deal of writing and preaching on the subject by those who thought deeply about death and had come to terms with it. One such effort is Jeremy Taylor's work, *Holy Dying*.

Writing in the seventeenth century, Taylor composed a sensitive, compassionate manual on the art of dying—"precepts and necessary preparatives to a holy death," as he put it.

Every event of our life is an intimation of mortality, he said. "At the end of seven years our teeth fall out and die before us," he wrote, and, the Tooth Fairy not withstanding, "represent a formal prologue to the tragedy."

Taylor works his way through our lives as age "takes our bodies, weakening some parts and loosing others." We taste the grave "as first those parts that serve for ornament and then those that serve for necessity become useless." Baldness, he said, is more than a blow to male vanity; it is "a dressing to our funerals, the proper ornament of mourning."

"Gray hairs, dim eyes, trembling joints, short breath, stiff limbs, wrinkled skin, short memory" are all reminders of impending death. "Every day's necessity calls for a reparation of that portion which death fed on all night, when we lay in his lap, and slept in his outer chambers. Every meal is a rescue from one death, and lays up for another; and while we think a thought, we die; and the clock strikes, and reckons on our portion of eternity." Thus we hear "the ticking of eternity"[39] in every stage of aging.

The problem, Taylor continues, is that death "seizes upon old men while they still retain the minds of boys and anxious youth. [They do] actions from principles of great folly, and mighty ignorance, admiring things useless and hurtful, and filling up all the dimensions of their abode with the business of empty affairs: they do not pray, because they are so busy; they do not attend to the things of God, because they are so passionate." *Driven*, we would say.

Taylor concludes by quoting Lucretius, the Roman poet: "The person is snatched away and the goods remain"—the exact point Jesus makes so eloquently in the parable of the rich fool.

Jesus' argument in the parable is that death came for the fool when he was busy about everything but the business of his own soul. He lived the "good life," but died badly because he was not "rich toward God." Thus he was unprepared.

Recently I came across a form for family evening prayer in a very old copy of *The Book of Common Prayer*. The prayer would be thought quaint today, and unsuitable for children, because of its candor about death and our need to prepare for its eventuality. But it too makes Jesus' point: "The family being together, a little time before bed time, let the Master or Mistress, or any other whom they shall think proper, say as follows, all kneeling, 'Make us ever mindful of the time when we shall lie down in the dust; and grant us grace to always live in such a way that we may never be afraid to die; *so that living and dying, we may be thine.*'"

Or, as Paul would say, "If we live, we live to the Lord; if we die, we die to the Lord. So, whether we live or die, we belong to the Lord" (Romans 14:8).

Holy living is the preparation for a happy, holy death. No other preparation is necessary.

> O eternal and holy Jesus, who by death hast overcome death, and by Thy passion hast taken out its sting, and made it to become one of the gates of heaven, and an entrance to felicity; have mercy upon me now and at the hour of my death; let Thy grace accompany me all the days of my life, that I may, by a holy conversation [lifestyle], and an habitual performance of my duty... be ready to enter with Thee at whatsoever hour Thou shalt come for me.
>
> — Jeremy Taylor

Malchus and His Kin

One proud lordly word, one needless contention. . .
may blast the fruit of all you are doing.
—RICHARD BAXTER

WARM-UP: *John 18*

I've often wondered why some non-Christians are so militantly anti-Christian, uncompromising and unreasonable in their hostility toward those of us who follow Jesus. Bashing believers seems to be their reason for being. It's an obsession that colors and controls all they think or say.

I suppose their antipathy could be nothing more than a desire for freedom: they'd rather fight than let their souls slip out of their own control. But even if they have chosen to take on their own souls, why do they need to take on Christians? Can it be that God has breached their defenses and gotten within their walls? When they rage at Christians, are they in fact raging against God Himself, whom they must resist with tooth and nail? I ask myself, "Who are they trying to convince?"

But the unbelievers who most touch my heart are those who've been wounded by well-meaning but witless believers who have hurt them with careless words or ways. Malchus comes to mind.

Malchus was in the band of soldiers who came to capture Jesus in the Garden of Gethsemane—the one, in fact, that Peter attacked. He was probably in the vanguard, showing particular zeal, for Peter would hardly have singled him out without reason. Peter took an awkward swing at his head and lopped off his ear, but Jesus at once stepped in, put an end to the conflict, calmed the crowd, and healed Malchus's bloody wound.

I've always wondered about Malchus. Did the two—he and Peter—know each other before this event in the garden? In those early days, Peter was not an easy man to deal with. Had Peter, at some point, inflicted a much deeper wound, which Malchus would not let Jesus heal?

Later in the evening a servant related to Malchus lured Peter into his second denial (John 18:26–27), and I've often wondered (though I do not know) whether Malchus fingered the big fisherman. Perhaps Malchus took his hostility to Jesus and His followers with him to the grave.

I recall a young atheist at a university where I used to serve, who fought with me, on philosophical grounds, for his unbelief—until in an unguarded moment he exposed the root of his resistance. When he was a child, he often thought about God and eagerly sought Him. One day a neighbor invited him to Sunday school, where the boy thought he'd surely meet his unknown God. Unfortunately, his neighbor forgot that he had offered the invitation and left the boy sitting on his front curb, scrubbed and eagerly "waiting for Godot," who never showed up. The man did not call to apologize. Nor did he invite the boy again.

The boy's disappointment turned to bitterness toward a God who was disinclined to meet little boys, and so he turned his heart away. The young philosopher's antagonism came not from his head, but from his heart. As Pascal observed a long time ago, the heart has reasons that reason doesn't have.

I knew a Malchus once.
Severely wounded by a Peter's sword:
crazed by anger, dazed by pain,
he thrust aside with awful pride
that Gentle Hand whose touch alone
could make him whole again.

"Have Jesus touch me? Hell!" he hissed,
"'twas his disciple swung the sword,
aiming for my neck and missed;
I want no part of Peter's Lord!"

Strong Savior Christ so oft repelled,
for rash disciples blamed!
Poor wounded fools, by pride compelled
to go on living—maimed!

—Ruth Bell Graham

I Spy!

You can observe a lot by seeing.
— Yogi Berra

This collection of stories, as I wrote in the beginning, is about ordinary people doing ordinary things in ordinary places. At first glance, there was nothing unusual about any of them, nor were their circumstances exceptional, except that God in some way or another was at work in and around them. It's what we learn about Him and His wise and gracious activity in each instance that gives meaning to each character's existence.

Their stories are ours, actually, for most of us enjoy similarly commonplace lives. We live on ordinary streets among ordinary people and we do ordinary things. Yet extraordinary things keep happening around us as a result of God's wisdom and grace—if only we have eyes to see them.

My wife, Carolyn, and I have friends who, when their children were small, played a variation of the game called "I Spy," the object of which was to see God at work in the common affairs of their world. If someone in the family saw God showing Himself in some way in their surroundings, he or she would call out, "I spy!" and all would be reminded of God's presence and creative activity in their lives.

I thought of that game as I worked on these stories, for in a sense I am playing "I spy." I am looking for, and presenting evidence of, God's activity in places where you would not expect to find Him.

I encourage you to do the same. All that it takes is a little time and a heart of love, for it is love for God that opens our eyes.

I'm reminded of John's account of Jesus' disciples and their futile fishing endeavor (John 21:1–7). Early in the morning they saw a man through the mist, standing on the shore. (They did not know it was Jesus.) "Have you caught anything, children?" the man asked. "No," they replied. "Cast the net on the right side," the man suggested. The disciples did as he asked and filled the boat with fish. "It is the Lord," John exclaimed. ("I spy!")

It was John, the man who fervently loved Jesus, who saw the Lord, an idea that greatly appeals to me. Love penetrates all of life, even those modest and mundane events in which we do not expect to find God. It enables us to see Him at work in the midst of common events, and what's more, to point Him out to those who do not see Him.

If you love Him, you will see His hand in the ordinary affairs of your life where others see nothing. Try playing "I spy!" ❧

Notes

1. From Sam Walter Foss, "A Friend to Man," *Best Loved Poems of the American People*, selected by Hazel Felleman (New York: Doubleday & Co., Inc., 1936, 1959, 36th printing).

2. Arioch, king of Ellasar, is known in ancient writings as Eri-aku of Larsa; Tidal, king of Goiim, was a Hittite king known as Tudhaliya; Chedorlaomer, king of Edom, was an Elamite king whose name appears in Akkadian documents as Kitur-Lagamer; Amraphel, king of Shinar, is unknown, but it's remotely possible he was the Babylonian law-giver, Hammurabi.

3. See Psalm 76:2. An Arab site within Jerusalem, *Silwan*, the Arabic equivalent of Salem, perpetuates the name.

4. Simon and Garfunkel, "The Boxer."

5. The devil hates our laughter. "Joy," C. S. Lewis's demon, Screwtape, writes to his nephew, "is a disgusting and a direct assault to the realism, dignity and austerity of hell."

6. Louis Smedes, in a sermon entitled, "The Power of Promises."

7. There is mystery here, for Jesus was fully God. Yet in the Incarnation He was fully man, and as such, He acted as a man wholly dependent upon God (cf. John 5:19, 30).

8. I recall Ernie Kovacs' acerbic comment that "medium" is exactly the right word for television since most of it is neither rare nor well done.

9. The Hebrew word *qubbah*, found only here in the Old Testament, is used in Semitic languages throughout the Near East for the inner sanctum of a "god tent."

10. One of George MacDonald's characters asks another, "Are you looking for something?" "No, just looking," is the reply.

11. His name, *'akan*, is taken from a Hebrew root, *'akar*, which means "a troubler of the worst sort."

12. I am greatly indebted to Dr. John White and his book *Parents in Pain* for some of the ideas in this essay.

13. Two texts suggest this idea. (1) 1 Samuel 16:11: When Samuel came to anoint the new king, Jesse, David's father, did not

include David with the rest of the brothers; and (2) Psalm 27:10: David's statement, "Though my father and mother forsake me, the LORD will receive me" is highly suggestive. The tenses in Hebrew indicate an actual rather than an hypothetical event: "Though my father and mother *have* forsaken me...."

14. "Tho' they may go a little wrong."

15. For the story of how the ark ended up at Kiriath Jearim, see 1 Samuel 6:1–7:1.

16. The Hebrew word occurs only here in the Old Testament and means "to twirl around."

17. The Hebrew text describes Doeg as "the chief herdsman," while the Septuagint adds, "he was a Syrian who tended Saul's mules."

18. The superscription of Psalm 52 reads, "When Doeg the Edomite had gone to Saul and told him: 'David has gone to the house of Ahimelech.'" The opening verses of the psalm suggest David's fury. "Big man," he fumes, "killing women, children, and defenseless old priests" (cf. vv. 1–5).

19. The word "kindness" in 9:7 is "covenant love," the love God has for us!

20. I am indebted to Dr. Howard Hendricks for this phrase.

21. The Greek of this text suggests a "purposeful" look.

22. From Handel's Oratorio: *Solomon.*

23. The same verb occurs in Exodus 36:7 where Moses asked the people not to bring more gifts to the tabernacle because "what they had was *more than enough* to do the work."

24. Compare John 6:11–13.

25. John White, *The Fight,* InterVarsity Press, 222.

26. Actually, most sexual predators are males. Since the Proverbs are written to a son, the predator is depicted as a female. But the proverb can just as well be addressed to a young woman who needs to heed this warning.

27. Isaiah includes the story of Hezekiah's decline to remind us that even the best of men will fail us in the end. There is no salvation apart from the Servant of the Lord (Isaiah 40–66).

28. The Sadducees may have taken their name from Zadok, whose name means "righteous one."

29. G. K. Chesterton said, "Great literature has always been allegorical—allegorical of some view of the universe." Poets, singers, story-tellers, mystics, and artists have always known this. This

approach to Scripture is valid, I believe, as long as (1) the spiritual is based on the literal, and (2) the spiritual expresses truth clearly set forth elsewhere in Scripture. These two principles prevent spiritual, symbolic interpretations from becoming uncontrolled and irresponsible. "They put a sober and scientific control on [them] like putting a strong rider on a strong horse" (Peter Kreeft).

30. Rabbi Jose bar Hanina, in his *Midrash on Psalm 23*.

31. Frederick Buechner, *The Hungering Dark*.

32. The verb *angareuo* ("forced") is a technical word, better translated "impressed." It referred to the legal right of Roman soldiers to conscript civilians for temporary service. The word occurs only in Simon's story and in Matthew 5:41.

33. The Christian writer Papias, who died around A.D. 130, tells us that Mark wrote his Gospel for the church in Rome.

34. I'm not suggesting that anyone submit to prolonged brutality and abuse, but only, in the words of the AA slogan, that we "accept those things we cannot change."

35. From *Experiencing the Depths of Christ Jesus*.

36. Simeon's song is known as the *Nunc Dimittis*, named from its first words in the Latin Vulgate translation, which mean "[You] now dismiss."

37. The phrase "no end" can be interpreted both temporally and spatially. The Moravian translation of this text is "without frontiers."

38. Dorothy L. Sayers, *Christian Letters to a Post-Christian World*.

39. Edna St. Vincent Millay.

Note to the Reader

The publisher invites you to share your response to the message of this book by writing Discovery House Publishers, Box 3566, Grand Rapids, MI 49501, USA. For information about other Discovery House books, music, or videos, contact us at the same address or call 1-800-653-8333. Find us on the Internet at http://www.dhp.org/ or send e-mail to books@dhp.org.